THE
POWER OF
POSITIVE
SELLING

Open the Door
and Close the Sale

DAN AND TRACI
SHOBLOM
STRUTZEL

MEDIA

MEDIA

Published 2020 by Gildan Media LLC
aka G&D Media
www.GanddMedia.com

First Edition: 2020

Front cover design by David Rheinhardt of Pyrographx

Interior design by Meghan Day Healey of Story Horse, LLC.

Library of Congress Cataloging-in-Publication Data is available upon request

ISBN: 978-1-7225-0314-7

10   9   8   7   6   5   4   3   2   1

THE
POWER OF
POSITIVE
SELLING

CONTENTS

Step Three

Close the Sale

Step Four

Parting Gifts

INTRODUCTION

In college, I worked in retail sales at The North Face, and my favorite customer interactions were always the ones when I'd recommend the customer go somewhere else. Don't get me wrong, I loved The North Face and all of their products. But I was always more intent on getting the customer the best product for what they were looking for. When that wasn't something from our company, I'd tell them what they should get instead, and where to get it from. Funny thing was, they always ended up buying something from me because they were so shocked that I wasn't just pushing our products on them. A great lesson I learned from this is that the best salespeople are the ones you trust.

—ANDREW PETERSON, CEO, SIGNAL SCIENCE*

Sales is considered to be one of the world's oldest professions. From ancient trade routes to modern Internet platforms, there are as many ways to sell as there

* John Brandon, "Eight Funny Stories for National Salesperson Day," *Inc.* (website), March 4, 2016, http://www.inc.com/john-brandon/8-funny-sales-stories-for-national-salesperson-day.html.

are people who buy things. But no matter what your product or service, who your target customers are, or whether you're a novice or seasoned salesperson, there is one truth that crosses all boundaries in selling: selling depends on a relationship. That relationship might last a few minutes, or an entire lifetime. But in order to conduct a sales transaction, there must be a relationship.

> *A sale is a transaction between two parties where the buyer receives goods (tangible or intangible), services and/or assets in exchange for money. . . . A sale functions as a contract between the buyer and seller of the selected good or service.*
> —INVESTOPEDIA

In any relationship, there can be problems. There's that relative who bores us with every single detail about his encyclopedic knowledge of cars, that coworker who is always trying to get people to invest in his cousin's network marketing business, that spouse who says, "You never listen to me!" Salespeople can make the same mistakes—talking too much, pressuring the customer to buy, or not listening.

Good sales relationships don't just happen. Like the others, the sales relationship needs to be nurtured and developed. You need to have solid communication skills and the ability to listen and understand what the other person wants and needs. You need to be able to compromise and negotiate. You need patience and persistence. Most of all, each person needs to have respect and trust for the other.

Sellers and buyers often have different perspectives. They each have certain needs and wants in the relationship, and those often can be at odds with each other. The key to successful sales, then, is understanding each side's perspective and bridging the gap to come up with a solution that satisfies as many needs and wants as possible.

The Power of Positive Selling: Open the Door and Close the Sale will help you do just that. You'll discover the key elements to creating and maintaining great relationships with your prospects and customers. Doing so will help improve your bottom line, but it will also allow you to add more value to your company and to the lives of your customers. Whether you sell a product or service as grand as one that saves lives or as small as a tiny part that goes into a complex machine, you will learn to make a positive impact on the world around you by what you do.

The Sales Cycle from the Salesperson's Perspective

Traditional sales books teach a sales process, which is a predictable set of steps that the salesperson goes through in order to make the sale. It is often represented by a diagram like this.

Meeting with prospect

Break the ice

Discover prospect's pain

Explain features and benefits

Overcome objections

Make the sale

While some elements of this sales process are useful, it represents only one third of the equation—the salesperson's perspective. It's "What can I do or say to get this person to buy what I'm selling?"

Example

Lisa is a sales clerk at a high-end makeup counter. Part of her sales process is to give free makeovers to customers who are visiting the counter. When a woman sits down for the makeover, Lisa has her as a captive audience for ten to fifteen minutes. First she breaks the ice. "Are you here doing some holiday shopping?" Then she identifies the prospect's pain. "What's your biggest beauty challenge?" She goes on to explain how her particular brand of makeup solves that challenge. If the prospect has objections, such as price, Lisa counters those. In many cases, she makes the sale. But as the customer walks away, only to be replaced by the next person at the counter, Lisa can't help but wonder, "Is there anything I could have done differently to make a better sale?"

The Sales Cycle from the Customer's Perspective

In truth, the customer often has a completely different process. That process has been called the *buyer's journey*, and it often looks like this.*

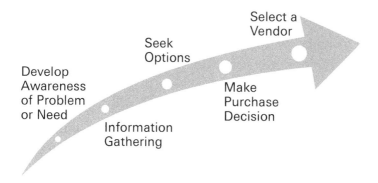

Develop Awareness of Problem or Need

Information Gathering

Seek Options

Select a Vendor

Make Purchase Decision

If you think about your own buyer's journey, you'll see that the salesperson (if there even is one) comes into the process about halfway in.

Example

Joan is going to a party where she'll see some former colleagues for the first time in several years. Not only has she gained a bit of weight, but she hasn't been sleeping very well. As a result, she has some dark circles under her eyes, and her cheekbones aren't as prominent as they used to be. She wants to look her best for the party, so she goes online to do some research. What can be done

---

* "What Is the Buyer's Journey?" Conductor.com (website), accessed May 24, 2020: http://www.conductor.com/learning-center/what-is-the-buyers-journey/

for circles under eyes? Is there a way to use makeup to make her face look thinner? She sees some interesting products online, and decides to go to the department store and see them in person.

While there, she meets Lisa, who offers to give her a makeover. During the makeover, Joan sees the products in action and decides to buy the undereye concealer from Lisa, but will get the face makeup online. As she's driving home, looking at her reflection in the rearview mirror, Joan can't help wondering, "Did I make the right choice by buying from Lisa?"

The customer's perspective is only one third of the sales equation. There is a third component—the relationship.

The Sales Cycle from the Relationship Perspective

From the early twentieth century until the present, the Avon Company has been a direct sales organization, characterized by "Avon ladies" (and men) who would go door-to-door selling cosmetics, perfumes, and other toiletry products. Before the advent of the Internet, when most shopping occurred in stores and markets, this was a novelty. Women would peruse catalogues, choosing items that they wanted to try. They would then call their local Avon representative, and the person would come to the home and demonstrate the products. Customers loved being able to smell perfume and try on lipstick before purchasing it. Perhaps even more important, though, was the relationship that developed between the representative and the customer. He or she often became part of the customer's extended family, and the selling opportunity became more like an anticipated meeting with a cherished friend.

It worked! At the time of this writing, Avon is the fifth-largest beauty company and the second largest direct selling enterprise in the world, with 6.4 million representatives.*

How has Avon maintained its status as one of the biggest sales organizations in the world for almost a hundred years? By understanding the power of the sales relationship. As with other types of interpersonal relationships, the sales relationship takes on a life of its own.

Here is what the sales cycle would look like if it were a person.

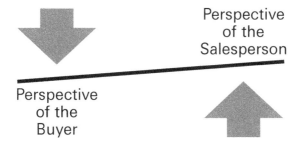

In other words, in order for the sales relationship to be balanced, it has to accommodate the perspective of both the salesperson and the buyer. If either one becomes dominant, the sales relationship topples.

---

* Beth Kowitt, "Avon: The Rise and Fall of a Beauty Icon," *Fortune* 165, no. 6 (April 30, 2012): 106–14.

Recently even Avon has struggled. Global sales fell for five straight years, and North American revenues fell 18 percent in 2014.* In 2016, Avon completed the sale of the remainder of its American business, meaning that all of its operations are now outside the United States. Given this, one has to wonder what has changed so much in the U.S. sales market.

The True Sales Cycle

If there are three components to our equation—the seller, the customer, and the sales relationship—then what is the true modern sales cycle? Surprisingly, it has more in common with event planning than a traditional sales cycle.

Here's what we mean. When an event planner is planning an event, there are four distinct phases. There's the *planning phase*, when the vision for the event is established, the venue and vendors are selected, and all of the other things that go into planning the event.

There's the *invitation phase*, when the guests are selected. The goals of the event determine who is invited. No matter what the event, the planner needs to make sure to invite the key stakeholders, and their needs and preferences have to be considered. If Aunt Beverly is being invited to the wedding, and she's vegan, the planner needs to make sure that there will be vegan food at the reception.

---

* Phil Wahba, "Avon's in a Ding-dong Battle to Stay in Business," Fortune, April 14, 2015: https://fortune.com/2015/04/14/avon-battle-for-future/.

Next comes the *event phase*. Executing the event flawlessly depends on the research and preparation done in the previous two phases. During the event is not the time to find out that there's going to be a routine fire drill, for example. The planner wants the event to go smoothly—not because he or she is trying to get anything from it, but because that's his or her job.

Finally there is the *follow-up phase*. Successful event planners understand that people have more than one event in their lives—and they refer new business. So developing an ongoing relationship is a key part of event planning.

The PPS Cycle

How does this translate to the sales cycle? This diagram illustrates what we're calling the *power of positive selling (PPS) cycle*.

This cycle emulates the event planning process, but in this case, the "event" you're planning is the sale.

First, the salesperson engages in planning, gathers product knowledge, thoroughly researches and understands his or her customers, and evaluates and manages the competition.

Then it's time to send out the "invitations," or communicate with leads. When it's finally time to open the door, the salesperson should have a clear understanding of his or her *own* needs and wants in the relationship. Next, as the sales conversation begins, it's time for the salesperson to build rapport and ask questions (and listen to the answers!) to develop the buyer's needs and wants. As the conversation progresses, the salesperson uses the power of stories to engage and persuade the buyer. Then, and only then, is it time to close the sale. This involves developing the offer based on what the buyer needs and wants, and crafting the "ask."

Handling objections and doubts is always part of the closing process as well. Since salespeople and customers can often be very different, it's important to handle that disconnect gracefully. All of these things occur *during* the sales conversation.

After the sale has been closed, the relationship doesn't end. To create a healthy sales relationship, the salesperson should be following up to prevent buyer's remorse and get feedback and referrals as well as testimonials. In addition, the salesperson should implement a system that allows for ongoing communication with the customer. After all, a relationship of any kind requires communication.

In the PPS Cycle, the "event" you're planning is the sale!

Here is more on each of the key components of the PPS cycle as it relates to the idea of selling as event planning.

Getting Ready

Getting ready to make a sale involves many things that salespeople are familiar with. Planning, knowing the product and its features and benefits, understanding your customers and their needs and pain points, and gathering information on the competition are classic functions of sales. But knowing all that information isn't enough. Like in event planning, the salesperson needs to be able to create an *experience* for the customer. It's not only about having the best product. It's also about the experience of buying.

Opening the Door and Closing the Sale

Clearly there is a huge difference between selling a five-course gourmet meal and selling a fast-food meal. Our point is not that the salesperson needs to roll out the silverware and candles in both events. Instead it's about understanding the needs and wants of both the seller and the buyer and finding the sweet spot in the middle. The seller clearly wants to sell his or her product or service. But the seller also wants a customer that's easy to work with, pays appropriately, and has other characteristics that make the sales experience easy.

The customer wants certain qualities in a salesperson as well. Some customers want a more customized approach, whereas others prefer to lead the sales experience. Understanding the needs and wants of both and adapting to them is the key to a successful sale.

Parting Gifts/Follow-up

Just as in event planning, the sale isn't over after the customer leaves the interaction. Following up is the most important element in the difference between a single sale and a selling relationship.

Have you ever gone to a restaurant, eaten a meal, and as you were leaving, been asked, "How was everything?" Often the manager asks that question because he or she is told to do so by upper management. But when the question is asked with genuine interest, it tends to build a positive feeling that makes it more likely that you'll go back, even if the meal wasn't perfect.

Similarly, calls, emails, and follow-up notes can keep the relationship going and make it far more likely that the customer will choose your business again.

The Power of Positive Selling addresses each phase of the PPS cycle—getting ready, opening the door and closing the sale, and parting gifts. In the rest of this book, you'll learn the most effective planning methods, discover how to handle rejection, develop your customer avatar, what to say to price objections, and how to create an automated follow-up system. This model isn't about pushing products or making people want to buy them. It's about building relationships based on trust and mutual respect so that people naturally buy from you because they like doing business with you.

As an illustration of the application of our model, we'll walk through it with a fictitious salesperson we'll call Scott. Scott is a traveling salesman who sells IT systems to businesses that are ready to switch to the cloud. We'll follow along as he applies the ideas and concepts presented in each chapter.

Step One
Getting Ready

Planning

Product
Knowledge

Customer
Understanding

Competition
Management

Seller's
Needs
and
Wants

Buyer's
Needs
and
Wants

Getting Ready

Opening the Door/
Closing the Sale

Parting Gifts/
Follow-Up

1. PLANNING

A door-to-door vacuum cleaner salesman manages to bully his way into a woman's home in a rural area. "This machine is the best ever," he exclaims, while pouring a bag of dirt over the lounge floor. The woman says she's really worried it may not all come off, so the salesman says, "If this machine doesn't remove all the dust completely, I'll lick it off myself."

"Do you want ketchup on it?" she says. "We're not connected for electricity yet!"

Eugene Wesson lost countless thousands of dollars in commissions before he learned an important truth. Mr. Wesson sold sketches for a studio that created designs for stylists and textile manufacturers. Mr. Wesson had called on one of the leading stylists in New York once a week, every week, for three years. "He never refused to see me," said Mr. Wesson, "but he never bought. He always looked over my sketches very carefully and then said: 'No, Wesson, I guess we don't get together today.'"

After 150 failures, Wesson realized he must be in a mental rut, so he resolved to devote one evening a week to the study of influencing human behavior, to help him develop new ideas and generate new enthusiasm.

He decided on this new approach. With half a dozen unfinished artists' sketches under his arm, he rushed over to the buyer's office. "I want you to do me a little favor, if you will," he said. "Here are some uncompleted sketches. Won't you please tell me how we could finish them up in such a way that you could use them?"

The buyer looked at the sketches for a while without uttering a word. Finally, he said: "Leave these with me for a few days, Wesson, and then come back and see me."

Wesson returned three days later, got his suggestions, took the sketches back to the studio and had them finished according to the buyer's ideas. The result? All accepted.

After that, this buyer ordered scores of other sketches from Wesson, all drawn according to the buyer's ideas. "I realized why I had failed for years to sell him," said Mr. Wesson. "I had urged him to buy what I thought he ought to have. Then I changed my approach completely. I urged him to give me his ideas. This made him feel that he was creating the designs. And he was. I didn't have to sell him. He bought."

—DALE CARNEGIE,
HOW TO WIN FRIENDS AND INFLUENCE PEOPLE

What Is Planning?

Every adult on earth has planned something at one time or another. Whether it's a matter of a simple afternoon outing or a complicated corporate strategy, planning is the art of getting from A to B.

Planning is the art of getting from A to B.

In sales, planning is an often overlooked yet critical step in the sales process. Too often salespeople simply learn a set of tools or techniques to sell their product or service, and then go out and try to sell as much as possible without having a structured plan for how to do it or identifying what the customer actually needs. Frequently it's not about building a relationship, it's about making sales. In this case, A can be thought of as "no sales" and B can be thought of as "making sales."

Traditional Sales Planning

In the story that opened the chapter, Wesson originally used a traditional sales planning model. He made sketches and then brought them to the stylist to see if he liked them. Here's how that looks.

Step 1. Analyze the status quo. "Where are we now?" ("What do I think the customer wants in a design?")

Step 2. Set sales goals. ("Sell one design to that client.")

Step 3. Develop the sales plan. ("Create as many designs as I can and show them to the stylist every week until he buys one.")

In traditional planning, you start by looking at the status quo: where you are now. In Wesson's case, he spent years creating 150 designs based on the status quo of what he *thought* the client desired.

Instead of the traditional planning model, a more effective technique is the feedforward technique. It's called *feedforward* because you look at the desired results in order to determine (or modify) the actions you take. In other words, you start by looking forward toward the end results desired.

> With feedforward, you start by looking forward toward the end results desired instead of where you are now.

The RAID Planning Method

One such feedforward planning method was developed in 1987 by management consultant and university professor Dr. Larry Pate, who was on sabbatical at the University of Queensland. It's called the RAID planning method, and RAID is an acronym for the steps.

R = Results desired

A = Actions necessary to create results

I = Indicators to watch

D = Decisions that remain

R: Results Desired

This is pretty straightforward. What results do you want to achieve? If it's a diet, how many pounds do you want to lose? If it's a sales situation, what results do your customers or clients desire? You don't start by looking at how many sales you want to make. You start by identifying the end result you wish to achieve, which is to achieve results for your customer.

In our opening example, once Wesson realized that he was failing to meet the needs of his customer, he changed to a feedforward method. He went to the client and asked what result *he* desired in a design.

In your sales, this might look like surveying, focus groups, interviews, and other methods that identify what result your product or service is trying to achieve. It can be as simple as, "I want a good hamburger for lunch," or as complex as, "I want a medical device that will save the lives of emergency room patients who come in with heart attack symptoms."

A: Actions Necessary to Create Results

These are the behaviors you need to engage in to gain the result. If you're dieting, it's the number of calories you need to eat and the number of minutes of exercise you need in order to gain the weight loss. Very often the salesperson will make assumptions about what he or she needs to do in order to produce the results the client desires. In Wesson's case, he was assuming that if he just kept making designs and showing them to the client, eventually one would work.

When that didn't work, Wesson changed it and showed the client incomplete designs and asked for feedback. Then the client told him what he needed to do by telling him what he wanted included in the design. He then knew what actions to take to get the sale.

In the A phase, you're not looking at what you're already doing. You're looking at what you *need* to do.

I: Indicators to Watch

Stacy loves to take road trips with her family. It's a great way to see new places. But she has a bad habit of disbelieving her GPS. Almost every time, about three quarters of the way to her destination, Stacy starts to think she is lost. "This doesn't look right. I don't think we're going the right way." Her kids then correct her by pointing out landmarks. "Look, Mom. There's the mountain that's shaped like a hand. We read about that online." They see indicators that tell them they are on the right path.

In the case of a diet, this phase is identifying the indications that you are taking the actions you iden-tified in the A phase, such as tracking your eating and exercise and weighing yourself. In Wesson's case, it was involving the client in the design process so that he would know that he was taking the correct actions to get to the results that the client wanted.

Ask yourself, "What indicators can I look for that will tell me that I'm taking the right actions?"

D: Decisions That Remain

This is where you finally look at the present. "What do I now need to do in the present in order to ensure that I can achieve the result?" In the case of a diet, how will you track and monitor your eating, exercise, and weight? What will you eat and where will you exercise? You need to make those decisions in order to take the actions that will lead you to the desired result.

In Wesson's case, it was a matter of asking, "How can I create a design that reflects the client's input so that I can include it to give him the result that he desires?" When one does this, the sale takes care of itself.

The customer is often the one who identifies the results desired and actions to take. The salesperson isn't always going to the customer with his or her ideas, but is instead finding out what the customer wants.

Of course, with some products and services, it's not feasible to ask each and every customer to be part of the planning process. If you're selling sweaters, for example, by the time the customer sees the sweater, the planning phase is over. The only customizable part at that point is color and size.

But using a feedforward technique like the RAID technique is an important first step in Getting Ready, because it enables you to create an action plan that leads to the results that the customer wants. Whether it's a perfectly cooked hamburger or the perfect summer beach home, RAID can help you set the stage for the sale.

SCOTT'S STORY

Scott Chapman loves his job as an IT salesman. He loves helping companies update their IT systems so that they can take advantage of everything that cloud-based technology can offer.

In the planning stage, Scott uses the RAID technique to plan his sales strategy.

R = Results desired
A = Actions necessary to create results
I = Indicators to watch
D = Decisions that remain

Results desired. What does Scott want? He wants to master the art of selling so in order to develop relationships with his prospects and customers that go beyond the initial transaction. It's not just about making one sale, but making many sales over the course of the relationship.

Actions necessary to create results. In order to establish a relationship with his prospects and clients, Scott will need to take certain actions. These include developing a customer avatar, researching their needs, communicating with the customer, following up, and other elements of a relationship.

Indicators to watch. How will Scott know that he's succeeding? The same way anyone in an interpersonal relationship knows: the level of engagement, body language, rapport, and ongoing sales are the indicators of whether Scott is succeeding.

Decisions that remain. What does Scott need to do now in order to ensure the result of mastering relationship selling? He needs to read on to the next chapter, which is about knowing your product or service.

2. PRODUCT KNOWLEDGE

A customer at Morris's Gourmet Grocery marveled at the proprietor's quick wit and intelligence. "Tell me, Morris, what makes you so smart?"

"I wouldn't share my secret with just anyone," Morris replies, lowering his voice so the other shoppers won't hear. "But since you're a good and faithful customer, I'll let you in on it. Fish heads. You eat enough of them, you'll be positively brilliant."

"You sell them here?" the customer asks.

"Only $4 apiece," says Morris.

The customer buys three. A week later, he's back in the store complaining that the fish heads were disgusting and he isn't any smarter.

"You didn't eat enough," says Morris.

The customer goes home with twenty more fish heads. Two weeks later, he's back, and this time he's really angry.

"Hey, Morris," he says, "You're selling me fish heads for $4 apiece, when I just found out I can buy the whole fish for $2. You're ripping me off!"

"You see?" says Morris. "You're smarter already."

*   *   *

Most of us have had the following experience in a restaurant: The waiter comes up and describes the day's specials in order to sell items that are either higher-priced than regular menu items or need to be sold quickly. Often the waiter's knowledge of the product determines whether or not you'll order it.

Scenario One

Waiter: The special of the day is a smoked salmon over a bed of microgreens served with a side of whipped sweet potatoes. Also we have a pasta dish with farfalle and sun-dried tomatoes in a mushroom cream sauce with grilled asparagus.

Customer: Oh, those both sound great. I was thinking of getting the crab legs, but I'm not sure. Which do you prefer?

Waiter: Those are popular items. I haven't personally tried them, but most people order the salmon over the crab legs.

Scenario Two

Waiter: The special of the day is a smoked salmon over a bed of microgreens served with a side of whipped sweet potatoes. Also we have a pasta dish with farfalle and sun-dried tomatoes in a mushroom cream sauce with grilled asparagus.

Customer: Oh, those both sound great. I was thinking of getting the crab legs, but I'm not sure. Which do you prefer?

Waiter: Well, it depends on your mood. The salmon is a smoky-flavored dish, and the whipped sweet potatoes are really light. So that's a lighter option, if you're watching your diet. But the pasta is rich and creamy and a bit of a decadent treat. And the crab legs are freshly caught, not frozen, so they are really sweet. We serve them with butter, but I actually prefer a side of hollandaise sauce to dip them in.

Now that your mouth is watering and your mind is thinking about dinner, let's take a closer look at both of those scenarios. In both, the waiter had a factual understanding of the product. He was able to describe the dishes literally: "This is what we are serving." When asked, he was able to tell the customer which of the dishes was more popular. Again, that's a factual piece of information. Those are *features*—the "who, what, why, when, where, and how" of a product. He is a perfectly good waiter. But there's a difference between a good salesperson and a great one.

Features aren't what sell products. Benefits are. It's clear that the waiter in scenario two had a greater level of knowledge about the food he was tasting and had actually tried the dishes. Because of this, he was better able to describe the benefits of the dishes. One was "lighter"; another was "decadent." If the customer is looking for a health-conscious meal, the salmon would be a better choice. If he is looking for something indulgent, the pasta fits the bill. The waiter isn't selling one item over another, but is describing the meals in terms of the benefits for the diner.

As a salesperson, the more you can master the knowledge of your product or service before you ever set foot in the sales environment, the more natural you'll be in conveying your enthusiasm.

Let's look a little more closely at the difference between features and benefits, as well as another thing to consider—advantages.

Feature: The factual information about a product or service.

Benefit: A brief, clear description of how a customer might enjoy or experience the product or service.

Advantage: The intermediary between features and benefits. They're how the feature becomes the benefit.

Example: GPS

Lee uses a navigation app on his phone to get around town. It has a crowd-sourced function, meaning that drivers can identify when there are road hazards, police officers nearby, or heavy traffic. That is a *feature*.

The *advantage* of this feature is that Lee is able to navigate around problems like traffic, road hazards, and police officers.

The *benefit* is that Lee gets to where he wants to be in the shortest amount of time and with less risk of an accident or a ticket.

The feature is a factual description of a product (crowd-sourced data). The advantage is how the user uses the feature to solve a problem (avoiding traffic). The benefit is the end result of the use of the product (saved time).

The key difference between features and benefits is that benefits have an emotional component that the customer can relate to. We may not know why crowd-sourced data is good, but we understand the frustrations of being stuck in traffic and the relief of being able to avoid it.

Transforming Features into Benefits

You want to have deep and extensive knowledge of your product service so that you can easily transform its features into emotionally compelling benefits. In essence, by describing the feature and then the advantage, you're actually getting the customer to realize the benefit on their own.

An umbrella that folds inverted is a feature. Staying dry when you fold the umbrella as you get in the car is a benefit. Streaming your favorite television series on your phone is a feature. Being able to occupy yourself while you wait somewhere is a benefit.

Now it's your turn. Here is a list of sample product features that *Forbes* magazine identified as the "hottest new car features for 2017."* What benefits come from them?

1. Automatic braking in dangerous situations
2. Automatic steering in dangerous situations
3. Forward collision warning
4. LED rearview mirror that shows a wide-angled rear-facing view
5. Full-blown onboard mobile computers
6. Live streaming TV in the back seat

Here are some of the advantages and benefits that come from those features.

1, 2, and 3.
Advantage: Avoiding a collision.
Benefit: Increased safety for loved ones and pedestrians.

4.
Advantage: Driver can keep an eye on the occupants of the car without having to turn around and looking over headrests.
Benefit: More security inside the vehicle. Ability to monitor kids.

---

* Jim Gorzelany, "The Hottest New-Car Features for 2017," *Forbes* (website), July 21, 2016: http://www.forbes.com/sites/jimgorzelany/2016/07/21/the-hottest-new-car-features-for-2017/#4bea90b375b8.

5.

Advantage: You don't have to use your tablet or phone to look up information. User-friendly interface.
Benefit: Quicker access to information. You are better able to keep hands and eyes on the road.

6:

Advantage: Being able to watch television while on the road.
Benefit: Keeping the kids quiet.

With a little practice, every one of your product's features can be turned into a benefit. Doing so will also help you better understand what your audience is looking for in a product and translate the features into the benefits that are particularly meaningful to your individual customers.

Now that you understand why it's so important to have a deep knowledge of your product or service, how can you find that information?

In an article in *The Balance*, author Matthew Hudson outlines several ways to do this.*

How to Gain Product Knowledge

• **Marketing literature.** Thoroughly read any marketing literature that comes with your product or service.

---

* Matthew Hudson, "How Product Knowledge Can Increase Sales," Small Business (website), May 23, 2018: https://www.thebalance.com/benefits-of-product-knowledge-2890302.

This is one of the best places to find the features.

- **Sales reps.** Ask other sales reps or your vendor about the product.
- **Training sessions.** Learn how to use the product. Few things are more embarrassing than trying to demonstrate your product when you don't know how to use it.
- **Testimonials.** What have other customers said about your product? What features did they like best? What benefits did they get?
- **Role playing** (the best system): Practice explaining the benefits and features *before* you get into the sales situation.
- **Practical use.** Go out to where your product is actually used and see how people are using it. You might gain some insight that isn't available from the user's manual or marketing materials.

It is important to understand how the product is made, the value of the product, how the product should and can be used, and what products work well together.

What to Know about Your Products

- Pricing structure
- Styles, colors, or models available.
- History of the product.

• Any special manufacturing process.
• How to use the product.
• Distribution and delivery.
• Servicing, warranty, and repair information.
• Most importantly, how to show what the customer is interested in.

In the next chapter, we'll look at the third of our four areas of planning—understanding your customers.

SCOTT'S STORY

In order to be able to effectively communicate the value of his product, Scott wants to be able to identify the benefits it offers to his customers. Here is his product: Scott's company, TechKNOWLEDGEy, Inc., converts a customer's IT system to software as a service (SAAS), using the cloud. Here are the features of SAAS:

• Web access to commercial software.
• Software is managed from a central location.
• Software is delivered in a one-to-many model.
• Users are not required to handle software upgrades and patches.
• Application programming interfaces (APIs) allow for integration between different pieces of software.

(continued)

But as we've learned, those are features, not benefits. So what are the *benefits* of using SAAS?

- Lower cost than installing on-premise software, because it's subscription-based.
- Easy upgrades.
- The ability to customize and scale to meet customer demand.
- Offloading applications like human resources (HR) and customer relationship management (CRM) to the cloud.
- Collaboration and communication between remote teams.

Now that Scott has a good understanding of his product and how it benefits his customers, he's ready to move on to the next step.

3. CUSTOMER UNDERSTANDING

The top toothbrush salesman at the company was asked by his boss how he managed to sell so many brushes. He replied "It's easy." He pulled out a card table, setting his display of brushes on top. He told his boss, "I lay the brushes out like this, and then I put out some potato chips and dip to draw in the customers." He laid out his chips and dip. His boss said, "That's a very innovative approach," and took one of the chips, dipped it, and stuck it in his mouth. "Yuck, this tastes terrible!" his boss yelled. The salesman replied "IT IS! Want to buy a toothbrush?"

It's January 2 of any year. Gyms are crowded with exercisers recommitted to getting in shape. Grocery carts are filled with diet foods, vitamin supplements, and food storage containers designed to help with portion control. The cover of virtually every magazine has a fit, healthy-looking model, and its inside is filled with products and services targeted to the health and wellness market.

Why? After all, people eat food every day. Many of us exercise regularly. We read magazines throughout the year. Why do marketers advertise so heavily to this specific market during that specific time of year?

The answer is obvious. In January, millions of people around the world buy these things because they are kicking off a health plan. Companies understand this, so they market their products and services to customers who want to buy health-related items. Since there are more customers at this time of year, there is more marketing to them.

It becomes a powerful cycle. People buy certain products, and companies realize this sales trend, so they market their products, which causes more people to buy those products.

In the previous chapter, we talked about understanding your product and how the features, the advantages, can provide benefits to your customers. But who exactly *are* your customers? Clearly not every product is suitable for every person. That's what we'll cover in this chapter.

Developing Your Customer Avatar

Customer avatar is a fairly new term in marketing and sales and appears to have been influenced by computer games. In 2006, an article in *Harvard Business Review* defined the term this way:* "Broadly defined, 'avatar' encompasses not only complex beings created for use in a shared virtual reality but any visual representation of a user in an online community."

Originally, the concept of a customer avatar was explored as a means for companies to market their products and services within the virtual worlds of video games and online communities.

The article goes on to say:

> Advertising has always targeted a powerful consumer alter ego: that hip, attractive, incredibly popular person just waiting to emerge (with the help of the advertised product) from an all-too-normal self. Now that, in virtual worlds, consumers are taking the initiative and adopting alter egos that are anything but under wraps, marketers can segment, reach, and influence them directly. Indeed, it's important for companies to think about more than the potentially rich market of the virtual world and consider the potential customer—the avatar.

---

* Paul Hemp, "Avatar-Based Marketing," *Harvard Business Review*, June 2006: https://hbr.org/2006/06/avatar-based-marketing.

That idea didn't catch fire, but the concept of an idealized avatar to represent one's target customer did. A quick Internet search of the term *customer avatar* brings up more than forty-two million results. Today *customer avatar* is defined as a fictional person who represents your ideal prospect.

A customer avatar is defined as a fictional person who represents your ideal prospect.

Why Identify Your Customer Avatar?

You might be thinking, "Why do I need to identify my customer avatar? I'm not in advertising or marketing; I'm in sales."

The answer is simple: in order to sell someone your product or service, you have to understand how it benefits them. Knowing your product is the first half. Knowing your customer avatar is the second.

The Ethics of Selling

Before we get into the specifics of identifying your customer avatar, let's touch on something that makes a lot of salespeople uncomfortable—the ethics of selling. Many people want to avoid the entire concept of selling because it seems smarmy: "I'm going to identify what you need so that I can sell you my product or service and benefit financially from it." When you look at it that way, it seems sleazy.

We aren't advocating that you identify your customer avatar so that you can manipulate someone into buying something they don't want or need. The premise of this book is *relationship* selling. As with any relationship, understanding the mindset of the other person is critical for its success.

In other words, you want to identify your customer avatar so that you can build a genuine relationship with the people who actually need what you are selling—the ones who really want to solve a problem and would truly benefit from your solution. There's nothing manipulative or unethical about discovering the psychology, needs, and wants of the people who would genuinely love to know about what you're selling.

Having cleared that up, let's move on to how to get very specific about your customer avatar.

The Two-Qualifier Method

Often marketing and salespeople are too broad or general about their target market. "Who would buy your product?" "Everyone." That's not true.

Ramit Sethi, author of the best-selling book *I Will Teach You to Be Rich*, elaborated on this problem in an email newsletter.

"The first question: Who are you trying to market to?"

The average person's response will sound something like this: "Well, you know, people who are interested in music." Or, "Uh . . . women!"

If this sounds like you, then you have joined 99 percent of other small-business wannabes who think they should target *everyone*.

That doesn't work.

To get your first three customers freelancing and go far beyond that, you'll need to learn how to target the right customers in extreme detail. With the right niche targeting, you'll be able to tailor and optimize not only your services but your pricing. When you target your services *specifically* to someone, truly personalizing it, they will pay virtually anything.

Targeting the right market isn't easy. Let's go through a quick example to set the stage. Imagine you've just been hired by a company that makes ski jackets and they say, "Help us reach more people."

Your first question is, "Whom are you trying to reach?"

They say, "Well, anybody. We just want to reach a lot of them."

You are doomed.

What's wrong with this approach?

Think about it. If you see a product that's just right for you, but it's also just right for your grandma and an eighteen-year-old kid, what are you going to do? Buy it?

Of course not. You're closing the window and moving on.

We want something that serves *our* needs, not our needs plus everyone else's. This is why men buy men's razors, even though cheaper women's razors would work just fine.

This is why certain restaurants can charge ten times as much as other restaurants. The food might be essentially the same, so what justifies the price difference?

To solve this problem, Sethi identifies the *two-qualifier method* for narrowing down your target market. In essence it looks like this:

[QUALIFIER 1] + [QUALIFIER 2] who need **[YOUR SERVICE]**

He offers three examples:

1. **Small-business companies** in the financial services industry who need copywriting for marketing materials.
2. **Bloggers** with 1,000 to 5,000 subscribers who want to develop information products.
3. **Working parents** in the San Francisco Bay area who want tutoring for their high-school kids.

In these examples, there are two qualifying characteristics as well as the product or service. In our opening example, we mentioned that marketers were selling to people who are on a health kick. But clearly that's not enough. Using the two-qualifier method, we would now say something like this:

- Middle-aged women who admire Oprah Winfrey who want to lose weight (Weight Watchers).
- Sedentary young men who watch sports and who want to get ripped quickly (Boot Camp).
- People who bring their lunch to work and are health-conscious and who want food storage that offers portion control (BeachBody Portion Fix).

How does your product or service fit the two-qualifier method?

You can have more than one customer avatar. It's perfectly fine to sell the same product to an eighteen-year-old kid and to your grandma. But you're not going to use the same selling technique, because these two customers have different avatars.

Five Components of a Customer Avatar

The online marketing community DigitalMarketer identified five components of the customer avatar:*

1. Goals and values
2. Sources of information
3. Demographic information
4. Challenges and pain points
5. Objections and role in the purchase process

---

* "The Customer Avatar Worksheet: Finally, Get Clear on WHO You Are Selling To!" DigitalMarketer (website), Sept. 3, 2019: http://www.digitalmarketer.com/customer-avatar-worksheet/.

We'll get into your role in interacting with these elements in the next section of this book. This chapter is all about your customers—who they are and what makes them unique.

Identifying these five components of your ideal customer will help you to become very specific about whom you are selling to. Let's look more closely at each of them, using a specific product—a college textbook for a leadership class.

Let's also bring back the idea that the customer avatar is an idealized version of a regular person, who wants to bring out the best in him or herself.

Advertising has always targeted a powerful consumer alter ego: that hip, attractive, incredibly popular person just waiting to emerge (with the help of the advertised product) from an all-too-normal self.

A Scenario

George is a sales rep for a textbook publisher. His job is to meet with business professors and help them identify the best book for their leadership classes. Although the professor doesn't actually purchase his or her own textbooks, by making it required reading for the class, he or she is responsible for the sales of hundreds of books.

The two-qualifier method: **College professors** who **teach leadership classes** who are **looking to adopt a textbook for their classes**.

George comes up with a customer avatar he's calling Larry. Here is how the five components look as applied to the customer avatar.

Goals and Values

What are the goals and values of your ideal customer as they relate to the product? Note that goals and values are different but related.

In this case, Larry has a goal of choosing the best textbook for his class. But even that is too vague. What constitutes the "best" textbook? This relates to Larry's values. Some textbooks rely heavily on case analyses, whereas others rely more on models and theories. Even those with case studies can often use old examples. Others update them more often. Some are very expensive, and some are less expensive. Some textbooks are available online, and others are not. Since George's textbook is available online, drastically cutting the cost for students, and has a lot of timely case studies that are updated every year, George is looking for customers who value these features.

Larry's goal. To obtain the best textbook for his class.
Larry's values. Inexpensive, online options, lots of case studies that are updated annually.

Sources of Information

Professors can learn about available textbooks from a variety of sources. They include campus bookstore offerings, unsolicited emails, campus visits with sales reps (either in office or as part of a group event), publisher booths at conferences and talks, word of mouth, and the Internet. Since George has an expense budget to travel to several leading conferences but doesn't plan to go campus by campus, Larry's avatar looks like this:

Larry's sources of information. Does *not* like unsolicited emails, attends talks and conferences on leadership, discusses textbook options with other leadership professors, and goes to his local campus bookstore to check out the titles available.

Demographic Information

This information will flesh out George's sense of Larry as a persona. Demographic information can include the following.

Age: 55
Gender: male
Marital Status: divorced
Number and age of children: four adult children
Location: Southern California
Occupation: business professor
Annual income: $100,000
Level of education: PhD
Inspirational quote: "The most important thing is to never stop questioning."

Other: He is an avid runner, a vegetarian, drives a sports
car, and loves to sail on the weekend.

Keep in mind that George will create other customer
avatars for different segments of his market.

Challenges and Pain Points

This area will come into play during the sales encounter. By clearly understanding what his ideal customer
struggles with, George will be better able to show how
his textbook's features will solve those problems.

Larry is challenged with:
- Finding a textbook that engages the students while
  teaching them valuable content
- Keeping the content fresh and relevant
- Alignment between the text content and the course
  material he wants to teach

Larry's pain points are:
- Fear of bad ratings from using a poorly constructed
  book
- Fear that his students will not learn the material
  from a bad textbook
- Fear of being embarrassed in front of other professors
  and his department chair by choosing a bad book

Objections and Role in the Purchase Process

In the final component, George must ask himself, "Why
would my customer *not* buy my textbook?" These are

the objections he'll need to overcome in the sales situation.

Larry's objections to the sale:
• The textbook might be too expensive.
• He might not want to update the book every year.
• Another vendor might have a better book.
• He may decide not to use a textbook.

Larry's role in the purchase process:
Although Larry doesn't buy the books himself, he is the decision maker. He will tell the bookstore to order the books and will require the students in his class to purchase it.

Other Avatars
Now that George has identified one customer avatar, it's time for him to create others. Each one represents a different sales opportunity. They might include the following:
• PhD graduate students who teach leadership classes. They are decision influencers who may go on to teach themselves.
• First-year professors
• Department chairs
• Corporate leadership trainers

The exercises in this chapter show us that getting a very clear idea of who your ideal customer is and what he or she wants from your product is a critical part of selling. Again, it's about developing a relationship that lasts beyond any single sale. That is what keeps your customers coming back again and again.

In the next chapter, we'll take a look at the final area in Getting Ready: competition management.

SCOTT'S STORY

In preparation for this sales experience, Scott realizes it's important to develop his customer avatars.

[QUALIFIER 1] + **[QUALIFIER 2]** who need **[YOUR SERVICE]**

Scott's customers are **independent medical groups** in **the Los Angeles area** who **need to convert their practices to SAAS and cloud-based IT**.

1. **Goals and values.** These clients value helping patients get the care they need, with frequent communication, quick processing of claims, and secure access to sensitive medical information.

2. **Sources of information.** Scott can get information on his clients through the Internet, through the American Medical Association, and through his colleagues.

3. **Demographic information.** They are usually younger doctors (under the age of fifty-five) with practices that have more than one location.

4. **Challenges and pain points.** Their greatest challenge is the speed with which technology advances and keeping up with it. Old software means patients will go to another doctor.

5. **Objections and role in the purchase process.** The decision maker is either the medical doctor or the office manager/administrator. One key objection is the need to retrain the staff on the use of Internet-based software. Initial cost, the security of sensitive information, and compliance with HIPAA privacy laws are also of concern.

4. COMPETITION MANAGEMENT

Two salesmen on a camping trip are walking through the forest when a huge grizzly bear appears in a clearing about fifty feet away. The bear sees the salesmen and begins heading toward them.

The first salesman drops his backpack, digs out a pair of running shoes, and frantically begins to put them on.

The second salesman says, "What are you doing? Running shoes won't help you outsprint that bear."

"I don't need to outrun the bear," the first salesman says. "I just need to outrun YOU!"

It's 2:25 in the afternoon, and Howard's phone alerts him that it's time to check-in for tomorrow's flight. He's flying to Atlanta to attend a conference. Last month, when he was making the reservations, he had several different airlines to choose from. In the end, he chose to book his flight on Spirit Airlines, the ultra-low-cost airline.

To keep airfare prices incredibly low, Spirit uses an ancillary service model, meaning that they charge separately for virtually everything. Baggage, advance seat selection, even the peanuts and soft drinks that other carriers offer for free, are all additional costs with Spirit.

As Howard squeezes himself into the cramped middle seat, he swears once again never to fly Spirit. Nonetheless, those low airfares are incredibly appealing. Chances are, the next time he needs to fly, Howard will choose Spirit over its competition.

Exactly *who* is Spirit's competition, though? And how does Spirit successfully compete against them, such that millions of travelers endure the inconveniences of ultra-low-cost flying just to save a few dollars? The answer lies in understanding one's *real* competition.

Four Areas of Competition

With any product or service, there are four ways in which a company can compete: *price*, *quality*, *variety*, and *convenience*. Most successful businesses focus on two or three of these. It's virtually impossible to lead the market in all four.

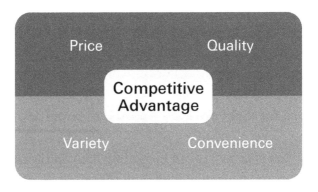

Let's take the example of a gallon of milk. If you are looking for the lowest price, you'll probably opt for a store brand at a big-box retailer such as Target, Walmart, or Costco. You might have good variety and quality, but it's less convenient.

If you're looking for the highest quality, you'll probably choose organic milk that you purchase at a boutique grocer like Whole Foods or Bristol Farms. The quality, variety, and convenience are there, but you'll pay more.

If variety is your primary goal, you'll choose a larger store with milks that have different levels of fat content, perhaps offering chocolate or vanilla milk, and maybe even nondairy milk options. You'll find variety and quality, but you'll probably pay more, and it may be less convenient to have to wander the aisle of a large store looking for a gallon of milk.

If you're more concerned with convenience, you'll probably buy your milk at a quick mart like 7-Eleven, but it will likely have higher prices and less variety.

Are those preferences static? In other words, do customers *always* choose the same one? Not necessarily. If it's two in the morning and your wife tells you that the baby needs milk, you're going to have to pay more for convenience, and you're not likely to find high-quality organic milk at the convenience store. Or although you might prefer to buy organic, locally sourced milk from grass-fed cows, you might not be able to afford it every time. If it's Christmastime and your budget is stretched, you might have to choose based on price rather than on convenience or quality.

So it's not good enough just to say, "We are the price leader" and focus on competing against other companies on the basis of price. There are other factors to consider.

Porter's Five Forces Framework

Business researcher Michael Porter identified five competitive forces that shape a business strategy.* While this isn't a book on that subject, a knowledge of these forces can help a salesperson better understand the competition. An in-depth examination of the framework is beyond the scope of this chapter, but here is a graphic representation of the five forces.

---

* Michael E. Porter, "The Five Competitive Forces That Shape Strategy," *Harvard Business Review*, January 2008: 86–104.

Let's look at them one at a time and see how they relate to sales.

New Entrants

Any industry that is profiting and doing well is going to attract new entrants. Look at the vegan food industry, for example. In the past few years, there has been a proliferation of companies offering vegetarian and vegan options. As more and more consumers are spending money on these foods, more and more companies are entering the market. If your product or service is one where there is high demand, you'll need to stay aware of new entrants in the industry. Your prospective customers will likely have heard of them, and to compete effectively, you'll need to know them too.

Substitutes

These are substitutes for your product or service. If a man goes to lunch and orders a soda, he'll likely be given a cup to choose his own drink. There are a series of selections for him to choose, and they are all substitutes for each other. To identify your competition, ask yourself, "What is the substitute for my product or service? If a customer were going to choose something else, what would they choose?"

Suppliers

Suppliers also influence the competitiveness of products and services. In our soda example above, one way that soda companies manage this competition is to create relationships so that vendors will only carry sodas in their product line. It's rare to walk into a restaurant and be able to choose either a Coke or a Pepsi; most places only carry one or the other. This is the negotiating power of suppliers. As a salesperson, it's important for you to understand the influence of this on your competitors. Maybe the competing product isn't available in a certain geography or at certain times of the year. Knowing how supplier influence affects your competition can give you a distinct advantage.

Buyers

These are the customers of the product or service you sell, and they have influence on the competition too. Group purchasing programs, such as auto clubs, can drive down the prices of certain products or services. Members can get discounts or special packages that are unavailable to nonmembers. As a salesperson, you might be able to use buyer influence as a selling point against your competition: "We have a loyalty club, and they don't."

Industry Rivalry

The first four forces contribute to and create the fifth force: industry rivalry. The intensity of this rivalry is a major determinant of how competitive an industry is. Said another way, the greater the other four factors, the greater the industry rivalry, and the greater the competition in the industry.

Competitive Rings

Another way to look at it is through rings of competition.

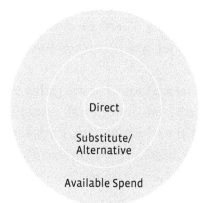

Direct

Substitute/
Alternative

Available Spend

Direct competitors are companies who sell the exact same product or service you sell. Domino's Pizza, Papa John's, and Pizza Hut are direct competitors.

Substitute/alternative competitors are similar products or services that are not direct competitors. A restaurant that sells pasta is a substitute for one that sells pizza. (That's why so many pizza places sell both.)

Available spend competitors are competing for the same dollars, but with a different product altogether. Instead of ordering dinner, a customer might choose to spend the same money on a movie.

The point of this analysis is to consider carefully, from the buyer's point of view, all the alternatives that there are to purchasing from you. In order to successfully compete, you have to have a thorough understanding of your competition. Where can you get that information?

How to Get Information about the Competition

Now that you know who your competition is, it's time to learn about them. There are two ways you can get information about your competition—primary and secondary.

Primary data are those that you gather yourself. Study competitors' ads, brochures, and promotional materials. Drive past their location (and if it's a retail business, make some purchases there, incognito if necessary.) Talk to their customers and examine their pricing. Learn what are they doing well and what they are doing poorly.

Secondary data are data that someone else has gathered. These include:

- Each competitor's market share as compared to your own.
- How target buyers perceive or judge your competitors' products and services.
- Your competitors' financial strength, which affects their ability to spend money on advertising and promotions, among other things.
- Each competitor's capacity and speed of innovation for new products and services.

In addition, certain facts might be specific to your industry. In our Spirit example, secondary data are things like on-time flight data, number of available routes, the age of the fleet, and things like that.

Finally, it's important to look at what your competition might be planning to do next. You can discover this by looking at the following:

- Annual forecast of sales, spending, and profits.
- Promotion and advertising programs.
- Introduction, support, and success of new products and services.
- Market, product, or service category and subcategory trends.
- Direction for future growth.

SWOT Team

All of this might seem like a lot of effort, but if you're to sell competitively, you need to fully understand your competition's strengths and weaknesses as well as opportunities and threats. In business, that's done by conducting a SWOT analysis. SWOT is an acronym for *strengths*, *weaknesses*, *opportunities*, and *threats*, and using this process on your key competitors can give you a selling advantage.

Strengths. These are the areas where your competition has an advantage over others. For Spirit airlines, one of the strengths of their key competitors is price. Frontier and Allegiant are also ultra-low-cost carriers.

Weaknesses. These are the areas where your competition is at a disadvantage relative to others. In the case of Spirit, the competition might not offer as many flight routes or flights per day.

Opportunities. These are elements in the environment that the competition (or you) might exploit. In the case of the airline industry, increased security measures can provide an opportunity. "We offer expedited boarding and TSA precheck." If your competition is offering something similar, you need to know about it so that you can counter it in the sales environment.

Threats. These are elements in the environment that can cause problems for your competition. In the case of airlines, changing consumer preferences is a threat. At the point where people like Howard are no longer willing to sacrifice personal space and comfort on a plane for price, some airlines at least will have to change how they sell their services.

Now that you've identified your competition and researched their strengths and weaknesses, you're better able to navigate the sales situation. But before you can actually get in front of your prospects, you have to be able to find them. That's what the next chapter will cover.

SCOTT'S STORY

Several other companies in the area help medical practices convert to cloud-based software. Scott needs to become familiar with them so that he can adequately counter any objections and questions such as, "Why should we go with you?"

Direct competitors include three other companies who do the same thing. When Scott conducts a SWOT analysis, he determines that because he is local to Los Angeles, he has an advantage.

Substitute/alternative competitors would be in-house software programs. Maybe the practice just wants to upgrade its existing in-house software instead of converting to the cloud. Or maybe they are considering outsourcing the functions completely.

Available spend competitors are competing for the same dollars. Instead of spending the money on SAAS conversion, the practices might upgrade their X-ray system, for example.

5. THE INVITATION:
Communicating with Leads

A tired traveler decided to find a hotel for the night. After checking in, he went to get some dinner and then went back to the hotel. But his room number wasn't written on his key. He stumbled to the front desk and said to the clerk, "Pardon me, I'm exhausted, I've been driving for fourteen hours, I'm hungry, and I have a headache. Can you just tell me what room I'm in?"

"Certainly, sir," the helpful clerk replied. "You are in the lobby."

Ruth is excited. It's finally the day of her party. She's cleaned the house, asked all of her friends what kind of food they like, chosen the date (working around the times and dates of other parties in town), made all the food, and gotten all the drinks. Everything is set. Except for one thing—where are the guests? Why aren't they here? Did Ruth forget something? Yes, she did. She forgot to send out the invitations.

Just like Ruth, you're ready. You've planned, mastered your knowledge of your product or service, identified your customer avatars, and have gotten insight into your competitive advantage. But unless you invite people to come to the party, there is no party.

Lead generation, or inviting them to the party, can differ widely depending on the type of sales you're in. If you're in direct sales (or multilevel marketing or network marketing), you need to have a different strategy for generating leads than if you're in retail sales. If you sell cars, for example, your dealership probably already has advertising, marketing, and guidelines for handling potential customers who walk onto the lot.

Even when you have a strong support system, you still need to constantly focus on where your next customer is coming from. It's the nature of the job. No matter how much organic traffic you get (whether in a brick-and-mortar facility or online), the more leads you have, the more sales you'll land. It's a numbers game.

This chapter will focus on how you can invite people into a sales conversation with you.

Locus of Control and Bias for Action

In psychology, there is a concept called *locus of control*. It's a mindset that reflects how much control a person feels about his or her ability to effect a specific outcome. Individuals with a strong internal locus of control believe events in their life derive primarily from their own actions: for example, when receiving exam results, people with an internal locus of control tend to praise or blame themselves and their abilities. People with a strong external locus of control tend to praise or blame external factors, such as the teacher or the exam.*

In addition, in the business world there is a concept called *bias for action*. Popularized by Tom Peters, author of *In Search of Excellence*, it reflects a propensity to decide or act without much analysis or sufficient information.

Generally, people who choose sales as a profession are more likely to have an internal locus of control and a bias for action. Otherwise the job would be too stressful. If you don't think you have much control over whether or not you make the sale, and you need to have a lot of analysis and information before acting, you're not going to be very successful in selling.

The link between an internal locus of control (a belief), bias for action (an inclination to act), and actually making a sale is in the actions that a person takes. In other words, you can't control whether someone buys your product or service. You can only control the actions you take that influence their purchase.

> *You can't control whether someone buys your product or service. You can only control the actions you take that influence their purchase.*

---

* N. R. Carlson, et al., *Psychology: The Science of Behaviour*, 4th Canadian ed., pp. 235-237 (Toronto: Pearson Education Canada, 2007).

KPIs

Every profession has a set of actions that, when taken, lead to success. They're called *key performance indicators*, or KPIs. KPIs are the activities you must perform to achieve success. They focus on tasks and behaviors that are easily quantifiable. In sales, some KPIs are:

- Number of appointments
- Number of trade shows attended
- Number of qualified leads
- Number of calls
- Number of repeat customers
- Hours of professional development
- Customer satisfaction ratings
- Social media interactions

Note that these don't include sales figures such as conversion rates or units sold. These are the behaviors that *lead* to sales.

Here are some of the other KPIs that are valuable to measure in sales.

Lead response time. A *Harvard Business Review* study showed that "U.S. firms that tried to contact potential customers within an hour of receiving a query were nearly seven times as likely to qualify the lead (which we defined as having a meaningful conversation with a key decision maker) as those that tried to contact the customer even an hour later—and more than 60 times as likely as companies that waited 24 hours or longer."*

Rate of follow-up contact. A National Sales Executive Association survey found that 48 percent of sales agents never follow up with leads a second time. This is significant, because 10 percent of sales are closed on the fourth contact, and 80 percent are made on the fifth to twelfth contact.†

Clicks from sales follow-up emails. This is about communicating something valuable to your prospects. (Some ideas are given later in this chapter.)

Social media usage. Research shows that LinkedIn and other social media are essential tools for effective sales.‡

Closing rate. Clearly, closing the sale is one of the more important KPIs. As we've said, you can't always control whether or not a prospect buys your product or service, but by measuring your closing rate, or what percentage of opportunities you actually close, you'll balance out the variables you don't control. If your close rate is low, you're probably doing something you can change.

---

* James B. Oldroyd, Kristina McElheran, and David Elkington, "The Short Life of Online Sales Leads," *Harvard Business Review*, March 2011: https://hbr.org/2011/03/the-short-life-of-online-sales-leads.

† Peter Radizeski, "Sales KPIs," TMCnet (website), Nov. 23, 2016: http://blog.tmcnet.com/on-rads-radar/2016/11/sales-kpis.html.

‡ Jesse West, "More Evidence That LinkedIn Is the Best Social Sales Channel," ringDNA (website), accessed May 18, 2020: http://www.ringdna.com/blog/linkedin-is-the-best-social-sales-tool.

Cold Calling Is Old Calling

Despite what a lot of salespeople believe, cold calling doesn't work. A recent study done by the Keller Research Center at Baylor University in Texas had fifty experienced salespeople sit down and make 6,264 phone-based cold calls over a two-week period.* Here's how it turned out:

- 72 percent of the calls were outright rejections: people saying, "No way," hang-ups, and so on.
- 28 percent of the calls were labeled as "productive." These were people who didn't hang up right away, showed some interest, gave a referral, asked to be called at a later time, and so on.

But what's most interesting is that the majority of the two-week study period was spent working on and following up with this 28 percent of the list. The time that went into it was extraordinary, and very eye-opening when you see the final results.

- That 28 percent, the "productive" calls, totaling 1,774, resulted in nineteen—yes, that's *nineteen*—appointments. Out of a total of 6,264 cold calls made!
- The success rate of cold calls to appointments is 0.3 percent (based on the average closing rate of 20 percent, that would equate to just under four sales, from 6,264 cold calls).

---

* Frank Rumbauskas, "New University Study Discredits Cold Calling," Business 2 Community (website), Jan. 3, 2013: http://www.business2community.com/marketing/new-university-study-discredits-cold-calling-0366600#HQERPke8elL6Iv2d.97.

Experienced salespeople can expect to spend 7.5 hours of cold calling to get one *qualified appointment!* Multiply that by the overall average closing rate of 20 percent in sales, and you're down to 0.06 percent. It's time to face the FaceTime. Cold calling is dead.

Just Take No (for an Answer)

There's a difference between persistence and pushiness. Just like that annoying guy at the bar who hits on every woman in the room and doesn't get the hint that they aren't interested, a salesperson who believes in the old adage, "Don't stop calling until you get a yes" is going to irritate and annoy a prospect into the arms of another, more respectful salesperson.

"A common piece of advice given to salespeople is to 'keep calling a prospect until you hear a no,'" said Mike Schultz, copresident of RAIN Group. "Well, let's say you are working hard at selling, and have a big pipeline with dozens or more people in it. There are bound to be some that have stopped responding."*

Reps who keep chasing their prospects until they get a no are wasting time and energy on people who aren't going to buy from them. They are also setting up a relationship where they can seem subservient to the prospect.

"You're the chaser," Schultz said. "They're the catch."

---

* "Don't Vomit on the Receptionist (and Other Bogus Sales Techniques)," Pipedrive (website), accessed May 18, 2020: https://blog.pipedrive.com/2016/02/ineffective -sales-techniques/.

A better idea, he said, is to send a frank message to the prospect after it's clear that the sales cycle has stalled, explaining that since the prospect hasn't responded, the rep assumes there's no interest and this will be the final contact. That message should also include contact information, in case the prospect would like to get in touch in the future.

"This works a lot better, because if they have moved on, you can too," Schultz said. "Even better, once some buyers realize you won't contact them again, they say, 'No, it's just been bad timing. Can we talk next week?'"

If a prospect tells a rep that they are happy with what they have, many reps will say "I can make you happier," author and sales coach Steve Schiffman says. Responses like that are knee-jerk reactions that won't help you close a deal, and can border on the obnoxious.

Overcommunication

Have you ever gone on a date with someone and found that they were far more interested in you than you were in them? Later, they kept calling, texting and posting on your social media pages. Did it make you *more* interested in them, or less?

Or have you ever woken up in the morning, checked your email, and seen that there were thirty-five new messages sent overnight, every single one of which was a sales email? Some companies inundate their email list several times a day with messages like, "This is your last chance!" You start to realize, "I am getting more emails from my florist than I get from my children."

Because it's so easy these days to be in constant contact with your prospects, there's a fine line to walk between being engaging and being irritating. If you find yourself sending out email blasts every day (or multiple times a day), tweeting and updating your social media constantly, and making nonstop follow-up calls, it's probably time to step back and rethink your strategy.

R.E.S.P.E.C.T. That's How You Sell to Me

As we've been saying throughout, the keys to a successful sales relationship are the same as the keys to any other form of personal relationship. It starts with a foundation of respect, and moves on to listening and having good rapport, as well as being sensitive to the other person. If you wouldn't drop in on your sister-in-law, refuse to take no for an answer from your spouse, or text or call your friends and family five times a day, why do it to your prospects?

Instead, *add value* to people's lives. Teach them something valuable. Brand yourself as an expert at whatever it is you sell. If you sell ice cream machines, teach people the best way to make ice cream. Write a book of ice cream recipes. Host an ice cream social in your neighborhood.

Here are some things you can do to offer genuine value to people so that they'll be more inclined to enter into a sales conversation with you:

- Training video series
- Free trials
- Webinars
- E-books
- White papers
- Bonus tips
- Interviews with experts on relevant topics
- Demonstrations and events
- Contests and sweepstakes
- Members-only sections on your website
- Personal coaching

So how can you use the concept of R.E.S.P.E.C.T. to become a better salesperson?

R. **Real.** Be real. Don't try to act "like a salesperson."

E. **Engaging.** Have an engaging personality. Be positive and uplifting.

S. **Supportive.** Be supportive and empathetic to the other person's situation.

P. **Personable.** Being personable means being easy to get along with.

E. **Energizing.** Bring energy to the meeting.

C. **Concern.** Demonstrate concern for the person and their company.

T. **Timely.** Respect their time by showing up when you are supposed to and leaving on time.

Front-End versus Back-End Sales

Now is a good time to mention the importance of not neglecting your existing customer base. There are three ways a business can increase revenue: it can raise prices for existing customers, acquire new customers, or sell something else to existing customers. It's like the older child who gets jealous and threatens to run away when his parents dote on the new baby. Make sure that you don't lose sales because you're more focused on getting new customers than on retaining existing ones.

There you have it. You've finished step one: Getting Ready. In the next section of the book, we'll get into the heart of the matter—the sales situation.

SCOTT'S STORY

Here are the KPIs Scott wants to focus on.

Lead response time. Communicating with prospects within an hour.

Rate of follow-up contact. Making sure he communicates with prospects at least five times.

Clicks from sales follow-up emails. Adding items of value, such as a newsletter or interview, so that prospects will engage with his follow-up emails.

(continued)

Social media usage. Scott commits to being active on LinkedIn and other social media five times a week.

Closing rate. He also commits to calculating his closing rate monthly and analyzing what he can do to raise it.

Here are some of the things Scott will do to add value for his prospects and customers.

- Training video series. An explainer video on the SAAS conversion process.
- Webinars. He can host webinars where doctors can ask questions.
- Interviews. He can interview an expert on a relevant topic and can interview existing clients on the newest software programs in medicine.
- Demonstrations and events. He'll host a monthly Taco 'bout It Tuesday event at a prospect's office, where he'll bring tacos and listen to their concerns about SAAS implementation.

Step Two
Open the Door

Planning

Product
Knowledge

Customer
Understanding

Companion
Management

Seller's
Needs
and
Wants

Buyer's
Needs
and
Wants

Getting Ready

Opening the Door/
Closing the Sale

Parting Gifts/
Follow-Up

6. KNOW THYSELF:
The Seller's Needs and Wants

Two shoe salespeople were sent to a rural village to open up new markets. Three days after arriving, one salesperson called the office and said, "I'm returning on the next flight. Can't sell shoes here. Everybody goes barefoot." At the same time the other salesperson sent an email to the factory, saying, "The prospects are unlimited. Nobody wears shoes here!"

Will never thought he would want to go into sales. He was a psychology major who considered becoming a police officer or a firefighter. But after spending a year in the Peace Corps, he realized that while he did want to help people, he didn't want to focus on people who were in a crisis. He wanted to be able to make a difference in the lives of regular middle-class Americans. He wanted to be able to offer them a product or service that he felt passionately about and would make their lives better in a discernible way.

So when he became a distributor for medical devices, he actually found it easy. His dad had a pacemaker that saved his life, and Will's passion for his product made it easy to connect with the doctors that performed that surgery. Taking a good look at his own needs and wants allowed Will to find a product—and a profession—that was in alignment with his values.

If you're reading this book, you've either already chosen sales as your profession or you're considering it. Have you ever asked yourself why?

As we mentioned in the introduction, in order for the sales relationship to be balanced, it has to accommodate the perspective of both the salesperson and the buyer. As in any interpersonal relationship, if either one becomes dominant, the sales relationship topples. If it is balanced, it's authentic.

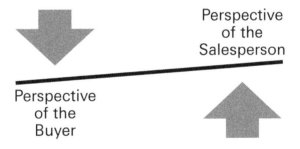

Perspective
of the
Salesperson

Perspective
of the
Buyer

What do you want and need from the sales relationship? The obvious answer is, "I want to make the sale so that I can have money." But let's look a little deeper. The transaction, or exchanging dollars for something of value, is only part of the relationship. There's likely to be a deeper reason you chose to go into sales and are interested in getting better at it. Like Will, you may have chosen sales for a deeper connection to a greater good. Or maybe you just like the freedom a sales job can offer.

Here are some reasons a person might choose a career in sales. Which ones resonate with you?

Money. With sales, you have more control over how much money you can earn.

A doorway into management. Many senior executives and managers started their career in sales. The skills learned in sales help at every level of the organization.

Personal control. You have more control over your time. You usually set your own appointments and have more flexibility over how you spend your day.

Career security. Almost every company needs good salespeople. If the company you work for goes under, you can take your sales skills and work for another company.

Personal values. You have the opportunity to express your personal values through the products and services you sell. Interested in animal rights? Sell vegan leather or meat substitutes. Are you an athlete? Sell athletic wear or fitness equipment.

Fun. Sales can be a fun job. You get to meet new people, travel, dress nicely, and have new experiences.

Psychological gratification. It is satisfying to close a sale. Whether you're selling someone their lunch or a new home, knowing that you've provided a positive experience and added value to someone's life can be psychologically gratifying.

Understanding your needs and wants in the sales relationship is a good foundation for successful sales. But there are still some roadblocks to consider: the excuses we tell ourselves about why we aren't getting the results we want.

Excuse the Excuses

Sometimes there are legitimate reasons for a setback. Getting a flat tire on the way to work because you ran over a nail is a reason to be late to work. But running out of gas on the way to work because you "didn't have enough time to stop" is an excuse.

Earlier we talked about locus of control. People with an internal locus of control avoid making excuses for negative outcomes. Perform a reality check here and ask yourself whether you are telling yourself any of the following things to excuse your behavior.

"I'm too busy." Every person on the planet has the same twenty-four hours in a day. Yes, some of us have more responsibilities and obligations than others, and those can be time-consuming. Instead of lamenting your lack of time, find a role model in someone who is busier than you but is still successful. Modeling after someone else is an effective way of mustering the motivation to keep going when you're overextended for time.

"I'm doing well. I can let up on my KPI actions." Now is *not* the time to let up! Your actions are exactly what is causing your success. You've found a formula that works, so stick to it.

"I'm too far behind to dig out." It's never too late. If what you've been doing isn't working, then it's time to adopt some new strategies. But the only person who ever actually fails is the one who stops trying.

"I don't want to lose the client, so I won't push." This is a tricky one, because it can be either an excuse or a valid reason. As we've said, sometimes it's best to accept the no and move on. But if you have a solid relationship with your client, you'll get an instinct for when it's time to gently push and when it's time to back off.

"It's not the right time" (holidays, summer, the economy, time zone difference, nobody is buying right now). While it's true that timing plays a part in sales, there are always people who thrive in every challenging circumstance. Some become millionaires right in the middle of a recession. In fact you can capitalize on the fact that other salespeople are telling themselves, "It's not the right time," and go out and land more sales.

"They can't afford it" or **"Our price is too high."** This is another tricky one, because it can be either a reason or an excuse. Clearly if you sell private jets and you're talking to a factory worker, they're not likely to be able to afford your product. But that's where identifying your customer avatar comes in. If you have clearly identified your ideal client as someone who can afford your product, then this is an invalid excuse.

"The competition is too strong." As we said in the competition chapter, sometimes competition *is* steep. But that just means that you need to take a look at their weaknesses and your strengths and find the sweet spot in the middle.

"It's not my fault. It's the company, boss, product, offer, marketing department, or bad territory." This is classic external locus of control thinking. While there may be limiting factors, such as a bad boss, poor marketing, or a slow territory, remember what we said about KPIs. If you keep taking consistent action, you'll get results. Or if it's truly something external, it might be time to take those killer sales skills and move on to a better environment.

"It's the buyer's fault" (the buyer is indecisive, is not the decision maker, has already made up his mind). This is another one that can be either a reason or an excuse. If you have vetted your customer well and have followed the key relationship selling principles and still don't make the sale, then step back and look at the big picture of the relationship. You may not have made the sale today, but you might down the road. However, if you're honest in frequently saying that it's the buyer's fault, then maybe you're not selling the right product to the right person.

"I don't have enough (money, connections, fill in the blank)." You don't. Unless you're Warren Buffett, you probably don't have the money and resources you'd like. But neither did he at first. It's about getting out there and doing the best you can with what you have until you have more.

"I'm trying my best." Are you? It's very easy to tell ourselves that we are trying our best. Keep trying harder! As Dale Carnegie said, "If you believe in what you are doing, then let nothing hold you up in your work. Much of the best work of the world has been done against seeming impossibilities. The thing is to get the work done."

"I can't handle rejection." This is a tough one, because no one likes rejection. It's human nature to want to be liked and accepted. However, in sales, rejection is part of the job. There will always be people who tell you no. You *can* learn how to handle rejection. The next section will show you how.

Getting to No

Rejection is part of the human experience. From nursery school to nursing home, being told no is part of life. It's not possible to avoid being rejected in life, and for some, it's the fuel that fires them on to greatness. For example:

- Michael Jordan didn't make his high-school basketball team. He was later named the greatest athlete of the twentieth century by ESPN.
- Marilyn Monroe was dropped in 1947 by Twentieth Century Fox after one year under contract because production chief Darryl Zanuck thought she was unattractive.
- Dr. Seuss's first book was rejected by twenty-seven publishers, and Seuss considered burning the manuscript. The eventual publisher sold six million copies.

- Barbra Streisand's Broadway debut opened and closed on the same night.
- Tom Cruise was rejected for a role on the TV show *Fame* because he wasn't "pretty enough."
- Walt Disney's first cartoon production company went bankrupt.
- George Lucas's first film flopped in 1971, prompting every major studio to turn down his next movie, *American Graffiti.*
- Steven Spielberg was rejected from the film school at the University of Southern California.
- Sylvester Stallone was thrown out of fourteen schools in eleven years. His professors at the University of Miami discouraged him from a career in acting. Stallone was also rejected for roles in the movies *Dog Day Afternoon*, *Serpico*, and *The Godfather*. His screenplay for *Rocky* was also rejected by all but one company, which insisted that if they bought it, he would not act in it.
- Billy Joel, embarrassed by his first album, *Cold Spring Harbor*, spent six months playing bar piano in the lounge of the Executive Room in Los Angeles under the pseudonym Bill Martin.
- Elvis Presley's music teacher at L. C. Humes High School in Memphis gave him a C and told him he couldn't sing.
- Jay Leno failed an employment test at Woolworth's.
- Billy Crystal was cut from the cast of *Saturday Night Live* before the show ever premiered.

- Barbara Walters was told to "stay out of television" in 1957 by a prominent producer.
- Clint Eastwood was fired by Universal Studios after his first two movies for talking too slowly.
- Lucille Ball was told that she had no talent and should go home from Murray Anderson's drama school. Failing to get into any Broadway chorus lines, she worked as a waitress and soda jerk.
- Van Halen's first demo tape was rejected by every major record label.
- John F. Kennedy lost the election to be president of his freshman class at Harvard. He failed to win a post on the student council as a sophomore and later dropped out of Stanford Business School.
- Thomas Edison was fired from his job working in a telegraph office after one of his experiments exploded.
- Dustin Hoffman, after failing to work as an actor in New York, worked as a janitor and an attendant in a mental ward.
- Benjamin Franklin attended school for only two years.
- Katie Couric was banned from reading news reports on the air by the president of CNN because of her irritating, high-pitched, squeaky voice.
- Mick Jagger was deemed "unsuitable" by the BBC to sing on the radio in 1962.
- John Grisham's first novel was rejected by sixteen agents and a dozen publishers. He later wrote *The Pelican Brief*, *The Client*, and *The Firm*, which were all best sellers and were made into movies.

- During its first year, Coca-Cola only sold four hundred Cokes.
- During his first three years in the automobile business, Henry Ford went bankrupt twice.
- R. H. Macy failed seven times before his store in New York caught on.
- General Douglas MacArthur was denied admission to West Point twice.
- Academy Award–winning writer, producer, and director Woody Allen failed motion picture production at New York University and City College of New York. He also flunked English at NYU.
- Albert Einstein didn't start speaking until he was four years old.
- Claude Monet had horrible cataracts but still became one of the world's greatest painters.
- Randy Travis was rejected by every major record label twice.
- Jerry Rice never made it to a Division I school to play College football. He later became the NFL's career leader in several receiving categories.
- In his first twenty years of business, Tom Monaghan went broke twice, lost control of his pizza company, and was sued for trademark violations. Later on, that company went on to become Domino's Pizza.
- Luciano Pavarotti could not read music, but went on to become one of the world's leading tenors.*

---

* Wayne Rickman, *Fair to Fabulous in Fifteen Minutes: Your Personal Journey to a More Inspirational Life* (Bloomington, Ind.: iUniverse, 2014), 80.

Clearly some of the most successful people to walk the planet have experienced and overcome rejection. But how? The answer lies in *frames* and *filters*.

Reframing Rejection

The book *Listen! The Art of Effective Communication* explains that when a sender and a receiver are communicating, they are doing so through frames and filters. A frame is, in essence, a broad, macro view of a given situation. It's as if your mind were unconsciously looking at things through a camera lens. It puts some things in and leaves other things out. A receiver can only hear or receive things that enter through the frame. Our frames are influenced by our gender, education, relationship with the other person, assumptions, personal agenda, sense of efficacy, and more. The experiences we have in the world, the things we learn and observe, all lead to frames.

Very often our frames are unconscious, meaning that we aren't always aware of how our experiences are shaping our perceptions. Your frame about rejection is influenced by the experiences you've had in society, in your family, and in your personal experience. Did you grow up in a community or family with external locus of control and unconsciously believe that there's nothing to be done about rejection?

While a frame is a big-picture view of a situation, a filter is a choice to focus more on one thing than another. Using the example of photography, the frame is what the camera lens can see. The filter is what it chooses to focus on: which areas are sharp and which are blurry? Which areas are light and which are darkened?

A filter is not a good thing or a bad thing. It's simply a way of managing all of the data that come into our minds. Our filters are the way we can change how we receive what someone is saying.

Our filters are the way we can change how we receive what someone is saying.

Therefore it's important to consciously look at the frame you have for sales rejection and what filter you use when you receive it. Then you can change the filter to one that allows you to experience rejection differently.

Rejection Assumptions

What are some of the assumptions salespeople make regarding rejection? What is the opposite assumption? Under what conditions would the opposite assumption be true?

1. I lost the sale because I'm a poor salesperson.
Opposite: I lost the sale *not* because I'm a poor salesperson.

Under what conditions would that be true? "Maybe it's not that I'm a poor salesperson, but that the customer didn't need my product at this time."

2. They bought from the competitor because their product is superior.

Opposite: They did *not* buy from the competitor because their product is superior.

Under what conditions would that be true? "Maybe it's not that the competitor has a superior product, but that it met one of the customer's other needs. What could that be?"

3. Once I've lost the sale, the customer will always reject me.

Opposite: Once I've lost the sale, the customer will *not* always reject me.

Under what conditions would that be true? "Maybe the customer will eventually realize that our product really will help them. What can I do to keep the door open?"

By identifying the assumptions you make about rejection, you can shift your filter from "I can't handle rejection" to "It's not personal, so I don't mind it."

In the next chapter, we'll finally open the door and let the customer in.

SCOTT'S STORY

As this chapter shows, Scott needs to understand his own mindset in order to succeed in sales.

Why did he choose sales? Scott chose to go into sales because it suits his personality. He enjoys the freedom to travel around Los Angeles instead of being stuck in an office all day. He gets emotional gratification from knowing that he's helping patients have a better medical experience. And he likes being an expert in something that doctors aren't.

What are some of his excuses? Some of Scott's excuses are that he is not a medical doctor and because of that, he doesn't understand their needs. He also feels limited by the geography of Los Angeles and surrounding cities. He can hear himself saying, "Traffic is terrible on Fridays. I won't get to their office in time."

What are some rejection assumptions he's making? In the event that Scott's prospects don't hire him, he tends to assume the worst: "I didn't explain it right." "They wanted to go with my competitor because they are a bigger company." But when Scott applied the assumption reversing technique from this chapter, he was able to see that the rejections were neither personal nor permanent. He just decides to go back and focus on his KPIs and trust the process.

7. BUILDING RAPPORT (The Don Draper Way)

A salesman was demonstrating unbreakable combs in a department store. He was impressing the people who stopped by to look by putting the comb through all sorts of torture and stress.

Finally, to impress even the skeptics in the crowd, he bent the comb completely in half, and it snapped with a loud crack. Without missing a beat, he bravely held up both halves of the comb for everyone to see and said, "And this, ladies and gentlemen, is what an unbreakable comb looks like on the inside."

In the critically acclaimed television series *Mad Men*, Don Draper (played by actor Jon Hamm) was the creative director of the fictional advertising agency Sterling Cooper. His character oozed charm, charisma, and business savvy. It was his job to sell the client on the advertising concepts that his team came up with. While he didn't land every sale (who does?), he exemplified the masterful use of rapport to convert skeptical prospects into paying clients. Here are some key lessons that we can take away from the show—even though it's set fifty years ago.

Research the Prospect before the Meeting

We've already talked about this in terms of a customer avatar. But in this case, we are referring to researching the actual person you'll be meeting with. Don Draper didn't have the advantage of LinkedIn or other social media, but you do. Before the meeting even begins, scour their social media to get a feel for what kind of person they are.

- Are they smiling in their profile picture?
- How are they dressed?
- What's the background of their photo?
- What kind of hairstyle do they have?
- Do they have an advanced degree?
- Have I been to a place they're from or went to school at?

This way, you'll have some starting ground for building rapport, and you'll be able to mirror the prospect more effectively. If the person is wearing formal business attire and everything about their profile screams "conservative," then you'll want to adopt that tone for the meeting. If, on the other hand, the person is wearing a Mark Zuckerberg–style hooded shirt and jeans, you won't want to show up to the meeting wearing a suit or a business dress. Don Draper understood this and would match his attire to the culture of the company he was pitching.

Get Your Prospect to Feel Emotion

Whether it's through nostalgia (like Don Draper showing his own family slides to Kodak in season 1), getting them to laugh (his drunken Life Cereal pitch), or getting them angry (his letter to *The New York Times* about the dangers of tobacco), stirring emotion is a great way to build rapport. From a psychological perspective, it causes the perception that you are both part of the same in-group. In other words, they'll feel more comfortable around you because they can relate to you and will have a greater level of trust.

Ask Relevant Questions

This is where your research comes in. If you've identified that the customer is a sports fan, is from a particular city, has a dog, or some other personal fact, ask questions about it. People love to talk about themselves and the things they are interested in. Find some way to genuinely compliment either the person ("Love your tie. My brother has one very similar. He calls it his 'lucky tie.'") or the thing they are interested in ("Your daughter has a black belt? That takes some serious discipline!"). Your interest has to be genuine. People can tell when you're trying to manipulate them.

Blogger Aja Frost offers these three general tips on asking good questions. They are:

1. **Personalized.** People tend to blow off questions like "What's the weather like?" or "Got any fun plans for the summer?" because these could be asked to—and answered by—anyone. If you ask a highly specific question, however, you'll show you're actually interested in the answer (and by association, in the prospect).

2. **Unique.** Your question should be a little unexpected. By catching the person off guard, you'll get a more honest answer— and research shows that honesty breeds intimacy.*

3. **Appropriate.** Even though your question should be surprising, it shouldn't be surprising in a bad way. Avoid anything that could be seen as nosy or out-of-bounds. For example, if the prospect says, "I just got back from a conference in Las Vegas," don't reply, "Nice! Did you get a chance to party?"

    Frost goes on to suggest several questions you can ask, broken down by category.†

Location Questions

• I see that you're in [city]. What's the best part about living there?

---

* George Graham and Hugh LaFollette, "Honesty and Intimacy," *Journal of Social and Personal Relationships* 3, no. 1 (1986): 3–18.

† Aja Frost, "Sixty-eight Memorable Questions for Establishing and Building Rapport with Customers," Hubspot (website), last updated Aug. 19, 2019: https://blog .hubspot.com/sales/instantly-memorable-sales-rapport-building-questions#sm.00 1y5drt8i1lcu7111913x5ppcsw4.

- Is it true what they say about living in [city/state]? (For example, "Is it true what they say about living in L.A.? Are the freeways essentially parking lots?")
- Since you live in [city/state], do you go to [local attraction] all the time?
- I have such good memories of [city/state]. I visited when I was X years old and absolutely loved [destination/feature]. What do you think about [destination/feature]?
- If I had the opportunity to pass through [city/state], what would be your top recommendations?
- Is [city/state] a good location for [prospect's industry/company/profession]?
- I've heard [nearby restaurant/city/state] has amazing [food item]. Does it deserve the hype?

Job and Career Questions

- My [niece/son/grandchild] wants to become a [profession]. Do you have any advice I should pass on?
- I saw that you used to work in [different field/profession/industry]. How was the transition?
- Do you go to [well-known industry event]? Why/why not?
- You tweeted about going to [conference]. Have you been before? I'm debating whether or not to go, and I'd love to hear your thoughts.
- My friend used to work at [current or former company]. Do you know [name]? What was it like working there?

- As a rep for [company], I talk to a lot of people in [prospect's profession], but you're the first I've met who's ever majored in [unexpected major]! How'd that happen?
- I read on your LinkedIn that you spoke at [event]— really impressive. Do you have any future speaking events lined up?
- I noticed you have your X certification. What was the process of getting that like?
- On your LinkedIn profile, you listed [unusual skill]. How often does that come in handy?
- You're fluent in [second language], right? Wow! Do you travel to [country] fairly often? Do you use [language] in your work? Is there a third language in your future?

School and Interest Questions

- You're an alum of [college]! My friend graduated from [college] in [year]. They said it was really X. Or, I've never met anyone who went to [college] before! What was it like? Would you send your kids?
- I noticed on LinkedIn that you help out with [organization]. How'd you get started with that?
- I saw on Twitter that you're a massive [sport] fan. Are you looking forward to [related event]?
- In your LinkedIn summary, you mention loving [activity]. How long have you been doing that?
- Just noticed you attended [school]. What was it like going to college [in the South/on the West Coast/in a big city/in a small city/etc.]?

- While I was preparing for our conversation, I noticed you follow [influencer] on LinkedIn. What did you think of their ideas on [topic]? (Alternatively, "Did you read their book?")
- I saw you follow [influencer] on Twitter. I do too. Did you see what they wrote the other day about [topic]?

Content- and Activity-Based Questions

- You recently tweeted a link to [podcast/radio show]. Have you listened to [specific episode/similar show]? (This question also works for books, movies, and TV shows.)
- I loved what you [blogged/shared] the other day about [topic]. Have you read [related article]?
- Since you're interested in [topic], I was wondering if you'd read [book on topic]?
- I saw that you tweeted about [author/book name]. I'm looking for a new read. Should I try [author/book name]?
- I'm putting together a list of great blogs for [prospect's industry]. Do you have any recommendations?
- I'm putting together a list of must-read blogs for any [prospect's profession]. Which ones do you like?
- I'm buying a book for someone's [milestone year] birthday. Do you remember reading anything around that time that really changed your life?

Company Questions

- Congrats on [recent company announcement]! How long was that in the works?

• I saw [company] won [award] recently—way to go! Did you submit an entry, or were you unaware that your team was up for consideration? Whom were you competing with?
• Your company just [opened up/moved to] a new office, right? What's the [neighborhood/city] like?
• I saw on Twitter [you/your company] just started using [noncompetitor product]. We were thinking of trying that one out. What's been your experience so far?
• Your company's retreat photo came up on Instagram. Did you like [destination]? What was the highlight of the trip?
• I was browsing your company's site when I came across the blog. I loved [your/your coworker's/your CEO's] post about [topic]; what do you think about [related topic]?

Random Questions

• I read on [LinkedIn/Twitter/your blog/etc.] that you think [opinion]. I feel the same way, but I'm always curious to learn how other people formed their opinions. How'd you come to this one?
• You seem to have a pretty busy schedule. Do you have any productivity tips?
• It seems that you're fairly busy. Do you use apps to stay organized? I've been looking for a good one, so recommendations would be helpful.

Know When It's Time to Get Down to Business

Don Draper had an instinct about when to cut to the chase and start the pitch. He did so by getting a feel for the room. Some clients need more time to talk and bond, whereas others want to get straight to the matter at hand. After you ask a question, stop talking and listen. At some point there will be a noticeable pause or lull in the conversation, and that's when it's time to move to the sales conversation.

The next chapter will delve into how you can identify the buyer's needs and wants through the power of listening.

SCOTT'S STORY

This is one of the easiest areas for Scott, given his naturally outgoing personality. When he researches the medical doctors before meeting with them, he can usually find one or more things they have in common. After all, Scott is Jewish and was raised on the East Coast, but went to UCLA. He loves the Lakers, has a Rottweiler, and his wife is a professional violin player. Scott makes sure to stay interested and aware of many different social topics so that he can easily

(continued)

talk to doctors. To that end, he reads up on the latest medical news ("Did you read that article in the *Times* about the heart surgeon?"), relevant political news ("I heard that the FDA is considering approving a new device for that"), as well as nonmedical topics ("My daughter is all aflutter because Beyoncé is having twins").

Today Scott is meeting with a prospective customer, Ed. He's an orthopedic surgeon who belongs to a larger practice of specialists. In the same office building are other physicians whose specialties range from dermatology to ophthalmology and internal medicine. Although Ed is at the same organizational level as the other doctors, they have tasked him with making the decision to hire a company to convert them to cloud-based software.

Scott's research tells him that Ed went to Ohio State, has a Golden Retriever, Lakers season seats, and is a board-certified orthopedic surgeon in Los Angeles.

As he walks into the office, meeting Ed for the first time, Scott has a lot of common ground for establishing rapport. "Were you at the Lakers/Cavs game last night? That was crazy! Were you always a Lakers fan, or were you a Cavs fan in college?" Before he knows it, they are talking like old friends.

8. THE BUYER'S NEEDS AND WANTS:
The Power of Listening

The entire North American sales force of Frisky Dog Food was gathered together for their national sales convention in Miami Beach. In the great auditorium the marketing director was giving a performance that any revivalist would have been proud of. Using the old pattern of call and response, he was really working up the spirits of his sales team.

"Who's got the greatest dog food in North America?" the marketing director asked.

"We have!" the audience replied.

"And who's got the greatest advertising campaigns?"

"We have!"

"Who's got the most attractive packages?"

"We have!"

"Who's got the biggest distribution?"

"WE HAVE!"

"OK. So why aren't we selling more of the product?"

One bold voice from the crowd replied: "Because the darned dogs don't like it."

*   *   *

"Hello, is this Ms. Vujicich?"

"Yes?"

"My name is Troy, and I'm calling from Sunbeam Solar. We're going to be installing solar panels in your neighborhood soon, and are taking a survey of residents to see how they feel about alternative energy. Do you have a few minutes?"

"I have a couple of minutes, but I need to get ready for work soon."

"Great, thanks. The first question is . . ."

(Five questions later) "OK, next . . ."

"Listen, Troy. I really need to get going."

"OK, no problem. But first, would you say that your interest in solar paneling is high, medium-high, medium . . ."

"No, seriously, I need to go."

"It will only take a couple of more minutes, and I need to finish this survey. Would you say your interest in solar paneling is high, medium-high . . . ?"

"Goodbye, Troy."

One minute later, the phone rings again.

"Hello?"

"Yes, it's Troy again from Sunbeam Solar. I really only have a few more questions."

"Troy, STOP. Go away!"

One minute later, the phone rings again. Ms. Vujicich doesn't answer the phone, and Troy keeps calling repeatedly. Finally she unplugs the phone. Ten minutes later, her roommate comes home.

"Why is the phone unplugged?"

"Some sales guy from a solar company keeps calling."

"I'll handle it."

The phone rings again.

"Hello?"

"Hi, may I speak with Ms. Vujicich?"

"She's not here. She's gone to work."

"Can I have her cell phone number? I'll call her on the way."

"I can't give you her cell phone number without her permission!"

"That's OK. If you give it to me, I'll ask her for permission when I call her."

"GO AWAY. STOP CALLING!"

While this scenario seems outrageous, it's an adaptation of an event that actually happened. This salesperson lacked one of the key skills needed for successful sales—effective listening. He didn't listen to the prospect when she said her time was limited. He didn't listen when she said she needed to go. Nor did he listen to her roommate telling him no.

Do you think there is any chance that either of these women will ever purchase from Sunbeam Solar in the future? Not likely. A bad experience like that can turn a person away from a company for life. Just because someone is speaking and you are hearing their words doesn't mean that you're actually listening and understanding.

Seven Types of Listeners

Not all listeners are created equal. In their book *Listen! The Art of Effective Communication*, Dale Carnegie and Associates have identified seven types of listener:

- Preoccupieds
- Out-to-Lunchers
- Interrupters
- Whatevers
- Combatives
- Analysts
- Engagers

The first six types are less effective than the seventh. Here is a more in-depth description of each type as they relate to sales.

The "Preoccupieds"

Sally is a classic "Preoccupied." While she is in a sales conversation and the prospect is answering a question, Sally is tapping her foot and looking at her watch. This gives the speaker the impression that she isn't giving her full attention and is just waiting to get to the next question. Preoccupieds come across as rushed. They are constantly looking around or doing something else. Also known as *multitaskers*, these people cannot sit still and listen.

The "Out-to-Lunchers"

Terry is an "Out-to-Luncher." When a prospect is speaking, he often finds himself mentally wandering or daydreaming instead of listening. These people are physically there for you, yet mentally they are not. You can tell this by the blank look on their faces. They are either daydreaming or thinking about something else entirely.

The "Interrupters"

Tracy is an "Interrupter." When the prospect is answering a question or commenting, she is just waiting for her chance to jump in and speak. These people are ready to chime in at any given time. They are perched and ready for a break to complete your sentence for you. They are not listening to you. They are focused on trying to guess what you will say and what they want to say.

The "Whatevers"

Carl is a "Whatever." He is physically present for the conversation, but he appears uninterested or bored. His body language and demeanor give the prospect the feeling that Carl doesn't care about what he is saying at all. These people remain aloof and show little emotion when listening. They do not seem to care about anything you have to say.

The "Combatives"

Peter is a "Combative." Hostile and rude, the Combative listener isn't listening for understanding. He or she is listening to get ammunition to use against the prospect to convince her to buy. These people are armed and ready for war. They enjoy disagreeing and finding flaws in logical arguments.

The "Analysts"

Carol is an "Analyst." These people are constantly in the role of counselor or therapist, and they are ready to provide you with unsolicited answers. They think they are great listeners and love to help. They are constantly in an analyze-what-you-are-saying-and-fix-it mode. While this might seem kindly, in reality it is a self-oriented listening style, as the Analyst is only filtering in information for which she has a "solution." She probably has no idea that her listening style is ineffective.

The "Engagers"

Finally, Lea is an example of an "Engager." These are the consciously aware listeners. They listen with their eyes, ears, and hearts, and try to put themselves in the speaker's shoes. This is listening at the highest level. Their listening skills encourage you to continue talking and give you the opportunity to discover your own solutions and let your ideas unfold. This is the cornerstone of relationship selling.

Your Key Question List

Now that you know the different types of listeners, it's time to develop a key list of questions that you can ask your prospect to further the sales conversation along. Here are a list of thirty questions developed by sales coach Sam Parker.* Which questions you use depends

---

* Sam Parker, "Top Thirty Open-Ended Questions," JustSell (website), accessed May 20, 2020: https://www.justsell.com/top-30-open-ended-questions/.

on where you are in the sales process. The most important key, though, is not the question you ask, but how
engaged you are as a listener.

Information Gathering

What prompted you/your company to look into this?
What are your expectations/requirements for this
    product/service?
What process did you go through to determine your
    needs?
How do you see this happening?
What would you like to see accomplished?
With whom have you had success in the past?
With whom have you had difficulties in the past?
Can you help me understand that a little better?
What does that mean?
How does that process work now?
What challenges does that process create?
What challenges has that created in the past?
What are the best things about that process?
What other items should we discuss?

Qualifying

What do you see as the next action steps?
What is your timeline for implementing/purchasing
    this type of service/product?
What other data points should we know before
    moving forward?
What budget has been established for this?
What are your thoughts?

Who else is involved in this decision?
What could make this no longer a priority?
What's changed since we last talked?
What concerns do you have?

Establishing Rapport, Trust, and Credibility
How did you get involved in . . . ?
What kind of challenges are you facing?
What's the most important priority to you with this?
What other issues are important to you?
What would you like to see improved?
How do you measure that?

By the time you're done with these questions, you should have enough information to see whether your product or service is a good fit for the prospect.

Tips for Effective Listening

Here are eight tips for effective listening.

1. Maintain eye contact with the person talking. If you're on the phone, close your eyes so that you can focus. Don't look at your computer or phone, or you'll get distracted.

2. Be sensitive to what is *not* being said. Observe body language for incongruent messages.

3. Practice patience. Do not interrupt, finish the speaker's sentence, or change the subject.

4. Listen empathetically and listen to understand. Act as if there will be a quiz at the end.

5. Clarify any uncertainties after the prospect has spoken. Make sure you understood what was said by rephrasing what you heard.
6. Don't jump to conclusions or make assumptions. Keep an open and accepting attitude.
7. Practice pure listening. Remove all distractions.
8. Turn off your mind and "be with" the speaker. Try to see things from his or her perspective.

Don't Answer Your Own Questions

Open-ended questions encourage prospects to open up and share information about their needs and wants. But be careful. It's easy to accidentally turn these open questions into closed ones. Don't start by asking, "What are the most important issues for you?" and then undercut it by suggesting answers, like promptness of delivery or price.

Never assume you know how buyers are going to answer. Ask your question and wait patiently for the response. Even if you have been in sales for years, don't make the mistake of assuming you know what the prospects' needs are. Let them tell you rather than you telling them.

In the next chapter, we'll get into what you should do when the questions have been answered and it's your turn to speak.

SCOTT'S STORY

In order to be an effective listener, Scott comes up with a series of questions ahead of time. This way he can focus on actually listening to the answers he's given, instead of thinking about what questions to ask next. As soon as he senses it's time to move on from building rapport with Ed, he starts to get down to business:

"So tell me what software you use most in the office."

"Do you use software to track physician referrals? Which one? What's your biggest challenge with that?"

"How long have you been thinking about switching to SAAS? What do the other doctors think about it?"

He tailors his questions to the kinds of answers that Ed is giving him, and it feels more like a natural conversation than an interrogation. But the way Scott was able to make sure of that was PRACTICE!

9. THE CONVERSATION:
The Power of Stories

A traveling salesman was passing through a small town in the West when he saw a little old man sitting in a rocking chair on the stoop of his house. The little old man looked so contented that the salesman couldn't resist going over and talking to him.

"You look as if you don't have a care in the world," the salesman told him. "What is your formula for a long and happy life?"

"Well," replied the little old man, "I smoke six packs of cigarettes a day, I drink a quart of bourbon every four hours and six cases of beer a week. I never wash, and I go out every night."

"My goodness," exclaimed the salesman, "that's just great! How old are you?"

"Twenty-five" was the reply.

Once upon a time, a farmer had a beautiful stallion, which helped the family make a living. But one day the farmer's young son left the gate to the stable open after cleaning it, and the stallion ran away.

His neighbors exclaimed, "Your horse ran away! What terrible luck!"

The farmer replied, "Maybe so, maybe not. We'll see."

Meanwhile, the stallion ran free over the hills and valleys, and came upon a band of wild horses. He joined them, and for weeks they all roamed the countryside, happy. One day, though, they came upon a hill that smelled familiar to our stallion. The scent of home-cooked food wafted into his nostrils, and the horse realized he was near the farmer's home. Eager to see his family, he began running in the direction of the farm. The other horses wondered where he was going, so they followed.

Seeing this band of horses running toward his farm, the farmer opened the gate to see what was going on. The horses ran in through the gate and onto the farm. Now instead of one horse, the farmer had a dozen.

His neighbors exclaimed, "Look at all those horses! What wonderful luck!"

The farmer replied, "Maybe so, maybe not. We'll see."

Curious, the farmer's son snuck into the stable late one night and took the most beautiful of the wild horses out so that he could ride it. But the horse was untamed and threw the young man to the ground. In fear, the horse trampled the boy's legs, breaking them both.

The neighbors exclaimed to the farmer, "Your son! His legs are broken! What terrible luck!"

The farmer replied, "Maybe so, maybe not. We'll see."

A few weeks later, the national army began rounding up all the young men in the village to fight in a conflict that had started a few villages away. But they did not take the farmer's son, as his legs were still broken. All of the young men were killed in the conflict, leaving their families grieving. "You are so lucky to have your son with you," the villagers said. "If his legs had not been broken, he would have been killed too. You are the luckiest man in the village."

To which the farmer replied, "Maybe so, maybe not. We'll see."

This Buddhist parable is often told to illustrate a powerful moral: things are neither inherently good nor bad. The farmer understood that things that look good or bad aren't either. They just *are*, and it's our labels that give things meaning.

Although the story does have meaning for us in a sales context (making or losing a sale can be either good or bad, depending on how you frame it), it illustrates the power of a story to convey a bigger idea.

Why Are Stories So Important?

Making sales presentations is a learned skill. Most of us can't just get up and do it without some basic training. The single best thing you can do for improving your presentation skill is to practice telling stories.

Why do so many people think selling is different from any other art form? No one would try to play the piano in public without years of training. Selling is no different, so taking the time to rehearse is an essential step. Rehearsing your presentation over and over again will greatly reduce anxiety. The more familiar you become with your material, the more passionate and convincing your presentation will become. The more comfortable you feel with your words, the more natural your speech will sound. That's why the best sales pros practice again and again. And that's why stories are so valuable. They're easy for you to develop and practice—much easier than memorizing a script.

Stories Are Powerful

Regardless of the topic, speakers need to be able to communicate persuasively with the audience. Whether someone is presenting data to a group of colleagues, offering a training session, sharing a case study, or making some other form of presentation, persuading the audience to see the key points is critical.

It's pretty clear why persuasion is important in sales. You've got to be able to persuade the prospect that your product or service is the best solution to their problem.

Stories are a way for presenters to keep the audience's attention while making the necessary key points. They are effective because people have been telling them since prehistoric times. People are familiar with them. Parents tell children bedtime stories. We watch stories on TV and in the movies. We read stories on social media. It's an important part of our experience as humans.

In addition, stories motivate people to take action because they tap into emotion rather than logic and because the hearers can see themselves in the characters, so the benefits (and pain) become more real.

Stories make all communication more powerful.

Why Do Stories Work?

Because people are accustomed to identifying with other people, a story will allow listeners to put themselves in the shoes of the person in the story. This can make the point much faster than if the presenter is simply explaining facts.

In research done for his book *The Hypnotic Brain*, Peter Brown demonstrated that stories synchronize the teller's and the listener's brain waves and enable similar areas of their brains to engage.*

Because of this, stories don't feel persuasive or manipulative. They're more like a virtual reality that is shared by the teller and listener.

Two Scenarios

Imagine two sales scenarios. Both salespeople are selling the same product to the same customer—a used car.

---

* Peter Brown, *The Hypnotic Brain: Hypnotherapy and Social Communication* (New Haven, Conn.: Yale University Press, 1991).

But one uses the power of storytelling to help make the sale, and the other uses traditional sales techniques.

One: Traditional Sales Technique

Salesperson: So tell me, Mrs. Smith. What brings you to the dealership this morning?

Mrs. Smith: Well, my car is on its last legs. I'm driving my kids to and from school, and my husband is actually taking the subway to work because we don't want to put any extra miles on the car. But I'd love to be able to have a reliable car and take him to work instead.

Salesperson: Oh, that sounds awful. I imagine you have to get up really early to do all that driving around. That has to be hard on your husband too. Let's see if I can help you get into a better car today.

Two: Storytelling Sales Technique

Salesperson: So, tell me, Mrs. Smith. What brings you to the dealership this morning?

Mrs. Smith: Well, my car is on its last legs. I'm driving my kids to and from school, and my husband is actually taking the subway to work because we don't want to put any extra miles on the car. But I'd love to be able to have a reliable car and take him to work instead.

Salesperson: Oh no! I had a customer once who was in a similar position. Her husband was a police officer, and because they were sharing one car, he took a graveyard shift so that they could share the car. He would take the car to the police station at night, bring it back at

6:00 in the morning, and then she would use it to take the kids to school and go to work. They did this every day for years, just because they had to share a car. By the time they came in to the dealership, their marriage was strained, and he was having health problems from working nights. And they never had any family time. I'm glad you came in before it got as bad as all that.

You can see how much more effective the second technique is. Instead of just getting the customer to identify a pain point (sharing a car), the second salesperson brought the customer into the life of another person who had a similar pain point, but had a much worse outcome. Mrs. Smith is going to be much more likely to solve her problem quickly as a result of emotionally connecting with another person with the same problem.

Go with the Flow

Even best-selling authors rarely establish the flow of their stories without many rounds of reorganizing. So after you've created your first draft and walked through a practice run, shift the content around until the flow feels natural and the presentation tells a compelling story. If you've backed up your key points with persuasive supporting content, such as industry statistics, quotes from analysts, or customer testimonials, you're likely to see a positive response to your presentation.

If you've backed up your key points with persuasive supporting content, you're likely to see a positive response to your presentation.

Elements of an Ineffective Story

We all know how to tell a story, but we don't all know how to tell an effective one. It's like the seven-year-old who tells a story but has to start over every time she is asked a question:

"I was on the playground today, and Susie came up to me, and she was crying."

"Why wasn't Susie in class? I thought she has a different recess than you."

"Her teacher was absent, so they were in our class today. So I was on the playground today, and Susie came up to me, and she was crying."

"Why was she crying?"

"Because Tommy stole her pencil. So, I was on the playground today, and Susie came up to me, and she was crying . . ."

You don't have to be a seven-year-old to tell a bad story. Here are some of the mistakes people make when telling stories.

Problems with purpose. There's no sense of why the speaker is telling the story to the listener.

Problems with focus. The story gives too much detail, begins too early, or goes on well past the point.

Problems with pace. Events unfold too fast, with little revealing detail, so it's impossible for a reader to make a movie in his or her mind; or events unfold way too slowly, with the key events buried among too many unimportant details.

Problems with engaging beginnings. The story begins with an information dump about the who, why, when, where, and how instead of having an effective hook.

Problems with conclusions. The story either stops cold or runs on, and the storyteller doesn't bring it back to the listener.

Developing Your Sales Stories

In his book *Unique Sales Stories,* author Mark Satterfield gives several excellent tips for creating effective and compelling stories that you can use in your sales presentations.*

---

* Mark Satterfield, *Unique Sales Stories: How to Get More Referrals, Differentiate Yourself from the Competition, and Close More Sales through the Power of Stories* (Dallas: Mandalay Press, 2010).

One: Determine Your Point for Telling the Story

The important first step in the process is to determine what point you want to make, what message you want to convey. Are you trying to establish rapport and break the ice? Then tell a story that relates to one of the topics covered in chapter 7. Are you trying to help the prospect feel his or her pain? Are you telling the story to show how another customer solved the problem? By identifying the reason for telling the story, you can make sure that your point is adequately conveyed.

Two: Follow the Structure

Every great story has a structure. A basic story has a beginning, a middle, and an end. In the best stories (1) a relatable main character (2) has a problem and encounters roadblocks (3) but emerges transformed, and the problem is solved.

Three: Create Sympathetic Characters

If your story has characters the reader or listener can relate to, the more attention they'll pay to what you have to say. (Not surprisingly, one of the best characters is yourself.) Choose stories with a character that is like your prospect. In our car sales example above, the main character had the same problem as the listener (sharing a car with her husband). Therefore you'll need to have a stable of stories so that you can choose the most effective one in the moment.

*Have a stable of stories so that
you can choose the most effective
one in the moment.*

Sales stories need to be about people to whom your prospects can relate. If you're selling insurance, a good character would be the victim of a flood or storm. If you're in the leadership advice business, the main character would most likely be an executive who is frustrated with internal communications, organizational silos, or corporate politics. In other words, the main character, the person who suffers from the problem, needs to closely resemble the prospect you're targeting.

Naming your characters makes your audience care about their problems. Remember, your readers and listeners need to be able to relate to the person if they are eventually to buy into your recommended solution. If you are creating sales stories in the business-to-business market, it's often a good idea to give an organizational title to your character. This not only adds a layer of context to the story but also sends a clear message about your target market.

Four: Establish the Problem

Great sales stories revolve around a problem—the gap between the current state and the desired state. That's what gets attention. That's what makes people say,

"Perhaps I should learn a bit more." It doesn't mean they're going to hire us. It doesn't mean they're going to give us money. But the right problem, presented in a way that is intriguing and compelling, can be the proverbial spark that starts the dry brush ablaze.

Five: Establish the Context

Next we need to combine the problem with context— the situation in which the story occurs. Leave this out, and you substantially increase the chances of losing the attention of your listener. In the opening moments of your story, the listener is not only digesting what you are communicating but deciding whether she wants to continue reading or listening. This is why an effective opening hook is layered with more details than one might initially expect. To do this, picture the event in your mind. Visualization is key for telling effective stories. Which leads us to the next tip.

Six: Use Emotion to Paint a Picture

In order to bring your listener into your story, use words that convey emotion. Words such as *frustration* and *fear* let us know about the state of mind of your main character. It's important to use language that is comfortable and natural to you and is also at the same level as that of your prospect. You'll have a serious disconnect if you speak above or below the other person's language level. (We'll get more into this in a later chapter.)

Seven: Use Consequences to Make Your Prospect Care

As we mentioned, every story you tell needs to have a point that relates to the sales conversation. You're not just telling a story to tell the story. You want them to care. How do we go from mild curiosity to having the prospect really care? By communicating the consequences of failing to solve the problem.

Consequences address the question, "Why should I care?" If the prospect doesn't care about the problem, they certainly won't care about the solution. If they don't, the odds of their becoming a paying client become very long indeed.

The more your story reflects the real world, the more credible it will be. In the sales story above, the salesperson mentioned that the other customer's marriage was in shambles, the husband's health had declined, and his relationship with his children deteriorated—all as consequences of sharing one car.

Eight: Bring It Back to the Listener

Of course the whole purpose of storytelling in sales is to get the prospect to understand that your product or service is the key to solving their problem. So you'll need to bring the conversation back to the listener.

The main objective is always to show your buyers exactly what you can do for them and to do that as convincingly as possible.

In the next chapter, we'll focus on the all–important offer and how to ask for the sale.

SCOTT'S STORY

Scott has developed three sales stories that he can use to communicate with his prospects. One of them is a rapport building story about when his uncle was in medical school, and a pizza delivery man arrived with his pizzas by ambulance.

The second story involves a benefit of SAAS. Scott tells a story about a plastic surgeon who had two female patients of the same name. One was twenty-five years old and had breast implants. The other was eighty-seven and had a cancerous mole removed from her face. Before converting to SAAS and the cloud, the surgeon's receptionist made an unfortunate error and emailed the eighty-seven-year-old asking how her breasts were doing. Now that the practice has converted to a cloud-based email system, mistakes like that aren't possible, because encoding makes sure that sensitive medical information isn't released to the wrong patient.

The third story counters a common objection—cost. Scott tells a story about a medical practice that was concerned that they would have to pay for their entire staff of 150 people to be trained in the new system. Scott mentioned that his company offers free training and that the office ended up saving money instead of spending it.

In the sales conversation with Ed, Scott tells the pizza story but not the one about the breast implant. His sense from talking with Ed is that the latter story is a bit too edgy, and Ed tends to be on the conservative side. Instead Scott tells about a dentist who had been missing referrals because of an unfortunate and inaccurate rumor that he'd passed away. "You don't refer business to a dead guy!" After a good laugh, Scott and Ed moved on to the next step of the sales conversation.

Step Three
Close the Sale

Planning   Product Knowledge

Customer Understanding

Competition Management

| Seller's Needs and Wants | Buyer's Needs and Wants |

Getting Ready

Opening the Door/
Closing the Sale

Parting Gifts/
Follow-Up

10. THE OFFER AND THE ASK

A famous art collector is walking through the city when he notices a mangy cat lapping milk from a saucer in the doorway of a store, and he does a double take. He recognizes that the saucer is extremely old and very valuable, so he walks casually into the store and offers to buy the cat for $2. The storeowner replies, "I'm sorry, but the cat isn't for sale." The collector says, "Please, I need a hungry cat around the house to catch mice. I'll pay you $20 for that cat." The owner says "Sold," and hands over the cat. The collector continues, "Hey, for the twenty bucks I wonder if you could throw in that old saucer. The cat's used to it, and it'll save me from having to get a dish." The owner says, "Sorry, buddy, but that's my lucky saucer. So far this week I've sold sixty-eight cats."

But Wait! There's More!

In the 1990s, one could hardly flip television channels without coming across an infomercial pitchman shouting at viewers. After showing us through laughable demonstrations ("Are you tired of _____?"), often showing people exploding, dropping, burning, or otherwise failing to use common household items like eggs, towels, or mops, the pitchman then goes on to show how his product easily deals with these difficulties ("Wait no more! The _____ can solve all of your problems!"). After shouting that the product is available "for three easy payments of $19.95" and that you can order it by telephone ("operators are standing by!"), to keep the viewer from changing the channel, the pitchman would usually throw in a bonus or extra offer by shouting, "But wait! There's more!" In addition to the main product, the customer could then get a variation on it ("handy travel size!") or an additional item for the same price ("Not one, but TWO!").

Although this technique is not commonly used today, it's become a humorous trope for overly aggressive sales offers. Yet every sales conversation needs to have both an *offer* and an *ask*. In our program *Sell Like a Pro*, we highlight the key elements of each.

The Offer

Communicating information about your product or service is called the *offer*. Every sale includes an offer. Sometimes that offer is very explicit. The salesperson simply tells or shows the buyer what the product or service can do and what the cost will be. In other instances, the offer becomes clear more gradually. The salesperson may never actually declare what it is. Instead it will become clear through the client's own answers to a number of carefully thought out questions.

The explicit offer. The salesperson simply tells the buyer what the product or service is and how much it will cost.

The implicit offer. The offer becomes clear as the buyer answers relevant questions.

Both methods can be effective. Which one is best in a given situation depends on the product or service and the personalities of the seller and the buyer.

In the past, the offer would be formulated for the salesperson as a matter of company policy. In smaller firms, the owner might simply tell the salespeople what to say and when to say it. Today most sales professionals are given more freedom about creating an offer to meet the buyer's criteria. Whether that freedom is a help or a hindrance depends on the skill of the salesperson. But the key is to focus on the benefits that match the buyer's specific needs.

What We've Learned So Far

As we've said, first, research the prospective customer to confirm a suitable fit with what you have to offer. In other words, you want to qualify or disqualify the buyer to the greatest extent possible before any direct contact actually takes place. By the way, these days, when Internet research is easy, buyers are going to know more about you than ever before (you didn't think you were the only one doing the research, did you?).

When you do meet with the client for the first time, you'll be in a position to quickly establish both personal rapport and your professional credentials. You can do this by telling stories about other clients for whom you've provided successful products or services. If you've done your research correctly, you'll be able to show how these relationships strongly resemble the new relationship you're developing here.

All along, ask open-ended questions to identify and explore your potential buyer's problems, difficulties, aims, challenges, goals, and possibly any unresolved issues. In short, reveal the pain that the buyer has been enduring without even being consciously aware of it. The client has been in pain, but was also so used to being in pain that he or she had come to accept it as inevitable. You're going to change that situation to the greatest possible extent.

As you create an overview of these concerns and needs on the part of the buyer, try to gain agreement on a single primary issue. This should represent both a major concern for the customer and a strong area of product or service opportunity for you. It could be an acute situation in which the buyer is engaged in firefighting right now. Or it might be a strategic opportunity for business development to which significant profits, savings, or competitive advantages are attached.

As the discussion continues, you'll want to clarify and quantify the effects of the customer's current pain as well as the positive opportunity you're now able to present. Simply put, what are the costs and negative effects of failing to resolve the present concern? Conversely, what are the positive effects and profits that will come from gaining a resolution?

At this point you're doing several very important things. You're revealing the real size and cost of the buyer's problems, which automatically heightens the priority and importance of those issues. This increases the buyer's feeling that action must be taken right away. It lifts your solution higher up the buyer's agenda and closer to the top of his or her to-do list.

Furthermore, by demonstrating the size and complexity of the buyer's needs, you also increase the opportunity for providing consultative advice. In other words, the customer has a stronger perception that your outside expertise is needed and should be paid for. When you show the high cost of continuing the status quo, you naturally increase the client's tolerance and expectations for the cost of your solution. As buyers realize the challenges they're facing, they'll accommodate themselves to the very fair price they'll be paying you.

Sell the principle that your solutions perfectly match the solutions that the customer needs—and that they also open new positive opportunities.

With major clients, the next step is often a survey or assessment of the present situation. That will lead to a fully detailed presentation, which can be presented by you or by your team. The audience would be the fully qualified decision maker(s) within the buyer's organization.

Buyers rarely explain everything to a salesperson during the first consultations. Sometimes that's because they really don't know everything, and sometimes it is just the nature of a buyer interacting with a new seller. That's why needs-creation selling is creative, in the best sense of the word, rather than manipulative. In short, customers and their organizations often need help, especially in the early stages of a sales relationship, with their processes of evaluation and assessment, decision making, communication, and follow-through.

Don't Give Away the Tacos

One danger in consultative selling is the temptation to give away too much help. When you go into a Mexican restaurant, waiters usually set down a bowl of chips and salsa to whet your appetite. It gets you eating, and the saltiness of the chips makes you thirsty (and more likely to buy a drink). But they don't set down a plate of free tacos. They're giving you the chips so you'll buy the tacos.

It's the same thing in sales. Only give enough consultation to tell the client *how* you would solve the problem. Don't solve it for them before they've committed to buying.

The Ask

When do you know when your prospect is ready to buy? Just like in any type of relationship, it comes from paying attention. Some indicators that your prospect is ready to buy include the following:

- Attention
- Relaxation
- Confidence
- Concentration
- Listening
- Enthusiasm

These can be observed through verbal affirmations, such as, "Sounds great!" "Looks good!" "I love it!" and "Count me in!" They can also be indicated nonverbally, by smiling, leaning forward, open body language, nodding the head, etc.

Just as the prospect can give you the signals that he or she is ready to buy, there can be warning signals as well. Here are some warning signals:

- Resistance
- Uneasiness
- Nervousness
- Impatience
- Anger
- Hesitation

These can also be indicated verbally ("I'm not sure about that . . ." "That doesn't sound right!" "I'm going to have to leave in a few minutes") or nonverbally (frowning, crossing the legs or arms, looking at the door, fidgeting, shaking the head).

By being aware of the signals you're getting, you'll know whether or not to advance the conversation to the ask or retreat to handle objections.

Don't Be Afraid of Commitment

The way to move forward from the offer is through commitments. Commitments are like punctuation points that organize a sales presentation and help it to go forward in an organized way. Your job is to get those commitments and to understand what they mean and don't mean. Here are some ways you can gain commitment all along.

Direct Question
Often the best way to gain commitment is to ask for it. "Are you ready to go ahead with this decision now?"

Alternate-Choice Method
Ask the customer to select one of two options. "Would you like one from the standard stock or one from our specialty line?"

Minor-Point Method
Call on the customer to make a minor decision indicating that the larger buying decision has been made. "In whose name should this title be drawn?"

Next-Step Method

Assume the sale has been made, and look past the commitment to the last actions that need to be taken. "When would you like for me to schedule the installation?"

Weighing Method

If the customer still has second thoughts about making the purchase, show him or her how the return on investment outweighs the cost. "Let's weigh the ideas causing you to hesitate and the value you'll realize from going ahead."

Depending on the prospect, you might want to use a story to convey these ideas. Some people might be put off by the directness of the above approach, so putting them in the context of a story can help ease the prospect's mind. "I had a customer once who preferred X, but his wife preferred Y, and he knew better than to come home without Y (laugh). Which one do you think your wife would prefer?"

Unfortunately, the vast majority of sales calls end without the salesperson ever asking for a commitment. This is a startling fact. It's amazing that anyone buys at all. It's also amazing how many more people would buy if requesting commitment were always a part of the sales process.

Commitment doesn't only mean asking for the order. It's much broader than that. It can be asking for the next meeting or setting a time for the next phone call or faxed document.

Commitment is simply moving the sale forward. Conversely, refusal to give commitment—or failure to ask for it— is a signal that the sale is in distress.

The next chapter will cover what to do if your prospect has objections or doubts.

SCOTT'S STORY

Scott has been in Ed's office for about twenty minutes. Things are going well. They've built rapport, and Scott has asked a series of questions in a conversational manner that let him know what Ed's needs are. Scott has a pretty good idea of how his solution can help Ed and the other doctors in the practice. Ed's body language is telling him that now is the time to move forward with the offer and to ask for the sale.

Scott says, "So from what I'm hearing, your biggest issues are tracking physician referrals, the need to share test results with both referring doctors and patients electronically, and automating the appointment system, including sending out pre-op paperwork and customer satisfaction surveys afterward. Is that correct? Am I missing anything?"

Ed then remembers that they want to be able to track expenses and give their accountant access to the data. As the conversation progresses, Ed refines his needs and remembers additional things that he wants.

Finally, after Ed has said, "That's pretty much it," Scott is able to craft his offer. "What we can do, then, is similar to what we do with other practices that have multiple specialties . . ."

He then goes on to describe the specific components of his service, making sure to match each item to a need or want that Ed has mentioned. Being careful to observe Ed's signals, he decides to do a trial close and ask for the sale. "Does that sound like something your group would be interested in?"

Ed leans back in his chair and crosses his arms, frowning slightly. "Well . . ."

Scott can tell that Ed still has some reservations.

11. OBJECTIONS, DOUBTS, AND DOLLARS

I had a door-to-door salesman call one time selling—of all things—burial plots. I told him that we already had our plots in another cemetery. He seemed uncertain about what to say next, but he recovered to say politely, "I hope you'll be very happy there."

I kept a record one time of more than five thousand interviews to try to find out why people bought or failed to buy. In 62 percent of the cases, the original objection raised against buying was not the real reason at all. I found that only 38 percent of the time did the prospect give me the real reason for not buying.

Why is that? Why will people—substantial people, perfectly honest in every other way—mislead and misrepresent facts to sales people? That's something it took me a long time to understand.

The late J. Pierpont Morgan Sr., one of the shrewdest businessmen in all history, once said: "A man generally has two reasons for doing a thing— one that sounds good, and a real one." Keeping those records for several years certainly proved to me the truth of this statement. So I began experimenting to find some way that I might determine whether the reason was real or merely one that sounded good.

Eventually I hit on a simple little phrase that produced surprising results and which has literally been worth thousands of dollars to me. It's common everyday phrase. That's why it's good. That phrase is: "In addition to that . . ."

—FRANK BETTGER, *HOW I RAISED MYSELF FROM FAILURE TO SUCCESS IN SELLING*

Common Sales Objections

It sounds like a bad date. "Sorry, not interested." "I've already got someone." "Just give me your number and I'll call you when I'm available." But these are some of the most common objections salespeople hear. In fact, here is a list of eighty-five of the most common objections:

1. Not interested.
2. Already have someone.
3. We are satisfied with whom we have now.
4. Don't need it.
5. We do it internally with our own people.
6. I can't use any more _____.
7. My boss won't authorize anything.
8. It will never get through the system.
9. I have to consult with _____.
10. That's not my area.

11. That has value, but not for me.
12. Home office requires that we use _____.
13. We have to use your competitor.
14. He/she isn't here anymore.
15. Just send me your literature.
16. Don't have time to discuss this now.
17. No one is paying attention to this area.
18. We'll muddle through.
19. It's too much hassle.
20. We won't use it.
21. No money budgeted; call me next year.
22. We're cutting back.
23. Not a priority now.
24. Timing's not right, see me next month or next year.
25. I need to think this over.
26. Too many things are in front of this.
27. It just won't work for us.
28. Never had good results with _____.
29. This isn't for us.
30. Don't want to stick our necks out on this.
31. You don't have what we need.
32. Your lead times are too long.
33. Management is taking a different track.
34. I need better quality than you offer.
35. We want someone in our own industry.
36. How do you know it will do that?
37. Never heard of you.
38. You're not large enough to handle the job.
39. I don't like your company.
40. I don't like your products/services.

41a. You don't understand our problems (insufficient diagnostic interview).

41b. You don't understand our problems (failure to present your situational analysis before the solutions phase of the presentation).

41c. You don't understand our problems (unfamiliarity with industry/company).

42. Your track record isn't strong enough.

43. Had a bad experience with your company.

44. That can't be done.

45. I don't believe it.

46. I've never heard of your company.

47. You'll have to prove that to me.

48. I've never heard about good results with _____.

49. Your _____ is not good enough.

50. We only buy name brands.

51. You don't have what we need.

52. Don't see any reason to change.

53. We've got to look at a number of suppliers.

54. Been doing business with them for years.

55. Not sure yours will work as well.

56. My brother-in-law is in the business.

57. Don't see any difference.

58. What makes you different?

59. Why should I buy from you?

60. We do it internally with our own people.

61. We want a Band-Aid, not a full workover.

62. Costs too much to change to your products.

63. We just like your competitor's product.

64. Not in the budget.

65. Your competitor does it for less.
66. Your price is way out of line.
67. Costs too much to change to your products.
68. I can't justify spending that much money.
69. My boss will never approve it (money).
70. Your price is too high.
71. We need a better price.
72. Can't afford it.
73. You'll have to do better than that.
74. Sharpen your pencils.
75. No one will use it.
76. Can't see how we could implement it.
77. Too much risk.
78. Change is tough to do around here.
79. Too much trouble.
80. They will never buy into it.
81. I'm not comfortable with this idea yet.
82. This is a lot to think about.
83. They will resist doing it.
84. We need time to adjust to this.
85. Don't know how to tell my supplier "no."

If you've been in sales for any period of time, you've likely heard several of these. Objections aren't something to run from or think about negatively. They are just part of the decision-making process. Think about the last time you purchased something. You likely had objections, reservations, or doubts. "The commercial said that this is a good brand of soap, and my sister swears by it. But will it work on Billy's soccer dirt?"

In fact overcoming objections can be one of the most interesting and positively challenging parts of the sales job. Mastering it can be the difference between success and failure in your profession.

> *The single best way to rise to the top of the sales profession is to become an expert at overcoming objections.*

In the list above, which are the most common objections to your product or service? Certainly money is likely to be the top one, but there will usually be five to seven others that come up repeatedly.

Reflect upon the sales calls you've made over the past year. What were the most common reasons people did not buy from you? Add what you come up with to the list if it's not already there.

Different Perspectives Lead to Different Objections

People buy from different perspectives, which depend on personalities and vary by function. Make sure you sell to people on the basis of their needs and their points of view. Keep in mind that in some situations, one customer will have multiple perspectives. Here is a diagram that illustrates four different perspectives of buyers.

Financial buyers are the ones who actually pay out the money for the product or service.

Executive buyers are the ones who are responsible for implementing the use of the product or service.

User buyers are the ones who will actually be using the product or service.

Technical buyers are the ones who are responsible for physically installing or setting up the product or service.

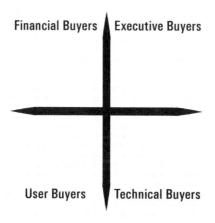

Financial Buyers | Executive Buyers

User Buyers | Technical Buyers

You can see that they will have different objections. For example, a financial buyer will be interested in cost, yes, but might also object to maintenance fees, upgrade expenses, and other things related to money. Contrast that with the user buyer, whose objections might relate to ease of use, accessibility, and other hands-on issues. The executive buyer might be concerned with what external stakeholders will think of the decision or with how widely accepted it will be across the organization. Technical buyers might wonder if they have the internal infrastructure to support the widespread implementation of your product or service.

Overcoming Objections

The first step in overcoming objections is to *create some level of cooperation between the buyer and yourself.*

You want the two of you to be on the same team working against the objections. This generally involves acknowledging that the subject is important and then getting the prospect to work with you to solve it. If the prospect says, "I need to think it over," you can say, "I certainly understand that: it's an important decision. Please help me understand what's of concern."

Cushions

In sales, these points of agreement are commonly called *cushions.* A cushion is a statement that shows the buyer you've heard the objection and understood its importance. Whenever a buyer states an objection, you should immediately cushion it. A cushion does not agree or disagree with the objection. It just assures the buyer that you've heard what's been said and you're treating it with respect.

Step two involves *getting all of the objections on the table before moving forward.* This will start to narrow the process toward a successful conclusion. Say something like "OK, we've identified that this is a concern. What other things do we need to look at?"

Objections are generally the result of two things: not enough information, or the wrong information. So your third step involves *finding out everything that you can about the objection, demonstrating the solution, and gaining agreement that the solution solves the problem.*

Value versus Cost

Any sale is a balance between *value* and *cost*. The buyer determines the relative importance of the items hanging in the balance. Your job is to change the prospect's perception so that value is equal to or greater than the cost.

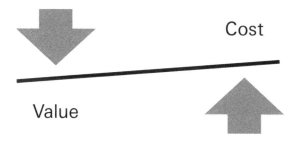

For instance, if a buyer says, "Your price is too high," you can demonstrate that the product is worth the price, or you can lower the cost. If a prospect says, "Your product doesn't have the feature I want," you can reduce the importance given to the missing feature, increase the importance given to other features, or some combination of the two.

Notice that all these options are focused on the nature of the product or service itself. There is nothing personal about this negotiation.

That's very important—and very difficult for many salespeople to grasp.

Some Objections Are Actually Obstacles

A final step is *identifying whether you're dealing with an objection or an insurmountable obstacle.* Sales pros like to think positively, but there is such a thing as an objection that can't be answered within your real-world situation. If the buyer needs a hydraulic lift to raise a fifty-ton object and the largest lift that your company can provide is rated at ten tons, no amount of sales expertise is going to move those extra forty tons. The best you can do is to create a relationship and move on to a more promising prospect. Conversely, those that treat all objections as insurmountable obstacles are also sorely mistaken.

When your customer states an objection, treat it with respect and listen carefully. Interrupting when you should be listening is a significant factor in the loss of trust and rapport. Even though you may have heard that same objection dozens of times, *avoid the temptation to start responding too soon.*

When you do begin your response, be sure that you understand your prospect's concerns very specifically. Otherwise you may sabotage yourself by addressing an objection the buyer hadn't even considered. It's a good idea to restate and gain agreement about the specific objection before responding. This not only provides clarity but also strengthens rapport.

Let's look at three general guidelines for dealing with objections, and then follow up with more detailed tactics.

Three Guidelines for Handling Objections

First, hear the objections out. Give the buyer your full attention and avoid the temptation to think about your response while he or she is speaking. Learn to be an active listener: not only listen to what the buyer is saying, but try to discover the deeper meaning behind the words. Since most human communication is nonverbal, pay attention to body language and listen for voice inflections.

Second, rephrase the objection for the buyer in the form of a question. This clarification gives the customer a chance to expand upon his or her concerns. It also reduces any perception of pressure. By having the opportunity to explain the problem, your buyer will frequently find the answer to his or her own objection.

Another reason for fully clarifying the objection is to make sure you are addressing the exact concern without creating a new one. Some objections are more important to your prospect than others. So after you clarify the objection, you need to ask your prospect how important that concern is to him or her.

Third, answer the objection. Make an effort to connect your answer with your unique selling proposition. Locate the objection within the big picture of your relationship with the buyer or the buyer's organization, and then narrow the discussion to create sharper focus. Try to get agreement from the client that the objection has been fully resolved, but recognize also that this isn't always possible. In that case, suggest that you'd like to give the objection some more thought and that you'll get back to the client about it in the very near future. Don't let the entire meeting get turned into a discussion of a single concern. If that happens, it won't be in the best interests of either you or your client.

Don't let the entire meeting get turned into a discussion of a single concern.

Gather as much information as you possibly can while the client is talking. At appropriate moments, ask questions to fully understand the objection. A good phrase is "Tell me more about that."

Don't Ask Why

On the other hand, if you ask a question that begins with "Why?" the prospect will feel called upon to reinforce all the reasons for their objection. This will only make it harder for you to respond.

Feel free to use open-ended questions of any kind, except those that start with *why*. As you ask questions, watch carefully for body language to give you feedback about what the buyers are really thinking and feeling. Keep your questions light and relevant. If you respond too aggressively, the prospect may feel closed to voicing any further objections.

When you're certain that the client has said everything that he or she wanted to say, *restate the objection in your own words.* Use an introductory phrase like, "I think I see what you're getting at." This will help ensure that you understand the objection completely. Restating the objection assures the buyer that you understand it and are taking it seriously.

If you have a strong response to a particular point that the buyer has raised, emphasize that point when you restate the objection. That way you will make a greater impression when you respond to it successfully.

After these two steps are complete—listening and rephrasing—you're ready to respond to the objection itself. This, of course, is a crucial transition.

Don't Argue

Just as you shouldn't manipulate buyers, you shouldn't directly argue with them either. There will be times when you're right and the buyer is wrong, but winning the argument—and embarrassing the prospect—ensures that you'll lose the sale. Never come right out and tell buyers that they don't know what they're talking about, especially when it's true.

Winning the argument—and embarrassing the prospect—ensures that you'll lose the sale.

---

*   *   *

The truth is, in any well-thought-out sales presentation, there are usually many more areas of agreement
than objections. By first giving attention to things you
and your buyer agree on, you can pave the way for a
painless discussion of key objections.

The power of this approach is so obvious that you'd
think more people would discover it for themselves.
But there's a strong tendency to feel defensive when an
objection is raised in a sales meeting. That tendency can
lead to a competitive or even confrontational tone in a
sales encounter rather than a cooperative one.

Always emphasize the positive before dealing with
any negativity the buyer might have brought up.

Be Specific and Concise

Avoid generalities when answering objections. Remember, the buyer has raised a particular concern. The only
way to resolve it successfully is to address it specifically.
Avoiding it will only cause the objection to stand out
in the prospect's mind as a reason not to buy. This is
an important principle of selling like a pro: *you should
never leave customers with anything they can regard as a
legitimate reason for not buying.*

Answer objections completely but concisely; avoid
too much detail. Use as few words as possible when
responding to the objection, and then return to your
presentation. Dwelling too long on an objection will
amplify its importance. Your answer should be just long

enough to satisfy the buyer. The objection will become more significant in the prospect's mind the longer you focus on it. And a long-winded answer will dilute the strength of your response.

You will often be able to anticipate and prevent certain objections that almost always come up. Make an effort to deal with them early in your presentation. This is much more positive than letting the buyer have well-worn objections raised over and over. But to do this, you need to be prepared.

Discover the deeper meaning behind the objection.

Hesitation

Unlike an outright objection, a hesitation is gentler. It's more a "pulling back" or a concern. But hesitation can quickly become an objection if not handled correctly.

When you hear a hesitation, your first instinct should be to cushion it. A cushion acknowledges that you have listened to the prospect, heard the hesitation, and recognized its importance. Remember, a cushion doesn't agree or disagree with a hesitation.

Hesitation: Your price is considerably higher than I expected.
Cushion: We hear that a lot.

Hesitation: I'm happy with my current provider.
Cushion: That is often the case.

Hesitation: I don't think we're ready to make a change at this time.
Cushion: That is a common response.

Don't use generic, overused responses such as, "I understand that is important to you."

Five Steps to Moving Past Uncertainty

After you've heard their hesitation, follow this five-step process to help customers move past their uncertainty.

Hesitation: My team is happy with the process they're currently using.

1. **Cushion.** A neutral statement that neither agrees nor disagrees. "We hear that a lot."

2. **Clarify.** Ask a nonthreatening question to clarify the hesitation. "Do you think they'd be willing to learn a new process that would . . . [major benefit]?"

3. **Cross-check.** Confirm that the specific hesitation is the only factor preventing the commitment. "In addition to this concern, is there anything else causing you to hesitate?"

4. **Reply.** Deny, admit, or reverse the hesitation.
   Deny. Deny falsehoods or misinformation.
   Admit. Admit current or past problems.
   Reverse. Turn objections into reasons for buying. "The process is easy to learn, and we'll help your team every step of the way."

5. **Trial close.** Ask a question to determine if the objection has been resolved. "Do you think your team would be OK with that?"

The Money Question

Of course, some of the most common objections revolve around money: "It's too expensive." "I can get it cheaper somewhere else." "I can't afford it."

Some salespeople falsely believe that money is never the real issue: "If you *had* to come up with this money in an emergency, you could find it." That's not always true. For some buyers, money really *is* the issue, and they actually do not have the money. If you're hearing this, however, you haven't done proper planning. You shouldn't be presenting to prospects who genuinely cannot afford your product or service. They should have been eliminated much earlier on.

Is Price Your Unique Selling Proposition?

Price should rarely be considered a unique selling proposition (USP), unless you're in a business where volume sales make radically lower prices the key feature. Our example earlier about ultra-low-cost airlines is a good illustration of a service where price is the USP.

Walmart is another example, and they put a slogan about low prices on the side of every one of their trucks. Low prices are the reason many people go to Walmart, and the nature of the company makes those prices sustainable. This is also true for ninety-nine-cent stores.

But for most sales pros, there are obvious drawbacks to making price your unique selling proposition. For one thing, although some people buy only the cheapest product or service, most don't. The majority of people will pay a little more or even a lot more to get a first-class product.

Furthermore, any product marketed with a low price as the unique selling proposition will always be vulnerable. What if someone offers an even lower price? And if you start being successful, you can be sure someone will.

The Price Is Right

When you encounter a price objection, start by looking closely at the price your buyer is referring to. Your price may indeed be higher than that of a competitor, but usually the difference is not substantial. Instead of avoiding the issue, call attention to the amount of difference.

Concede that your price is higher. But point out that while the actual difference in price may be only something like 15 percent, the buyer will get much more than that in terms of features, capacity, or performance with your product or service. *Make these benefits very clear.*

Be sure to explain how *the purchase is not an expense but an investment.* Show the buyer in detail how much he or she can benefit in terms of savings or profit. Contrast this with the small additional amount your product may actually cost.

Break the price down into smaller units. Clarify how small the actual price of the product is by showing what it would cost per day, week, or year over the life of the product. Even buyers on very tight budgets can afford pennies a day to reach their goals.

Mention the fact that in the real world *people get what they pay for.* Ask the buyer to recall a purchase based on a low price that he or she has regretted. Almost everyone has a story to support this principle. This is also a good time to bring in a story of your own if the buyer can't immediately think of one.

Compare the price of your product with others in the same marketplace. Just as some competitors may be cheaper, others probably cost more as well. Show how your product or service offers features found in much more expensive competitors. This will make your price seem less significant and will build perceived value. Be sure to compare results, not just price.

Remind your buyers that what really matters are the results a product or service delivers, not just what was paid for it. Call attention to the secondary benefits of dealing with you and your company. Explain to the buyer that the price you quote reflects the total value received, including other benefits, such as dependable service. Emphasize your unique selling proposition. Mention features of your product that are different and better than the competition's. Many products may look alike and may seem just as good as one another, but in reality they can be very different. Be sure to point this out.

Whenever a buyer says, "Your price is too high," you should immediately cushion and address the objection.

What Not to Say

You should avoid using the following responses:

- "Are you more concerned with price than value?"
- "Our prices may be higher—but considering the quality of what we offer, the difference should be much greater. You get what you pay for."
- "You can always pay less, but will you be getting the quality you want? That's highly doubtful."
- "Prices are not the same, because quality and service are not the same."

If your listeners aren't ready to make a decision at the end of your presentation, schedule another appointment. Come up with a reason to get back in there.

In the next chapter, we'll talk about what to do when your buyer is different from you in some key way.

SCOTT'S STORY

When we last left Ed and Scott, Scott was starting to sense that Ed had some hesitation. Immediately he addressed it: "I'm sensing some reservation. Do you mind sharing your concerns?"

"We have quite a bit of turnover in our staff. Not that people get upset with us, but often interns and residents come for a specified period of time and then leave. I'm concerned about constantly training new people to use your system."

"We specialize in medical groups, so we hear that a lot. We actually have a program where, at no extra cost, we'll come out for half a day and walk any new people through how to use the system. It's also a good refresher for anyone who may have forgotten. Plus, when we roll out a major software upgrade, we'll schedule a workshop. And we bring the pizza—which makes us very popular."

Both men laugh.

Scott goes on to say, "What else? What other concerns do you have?"

Ed replies, "Well, our radiologist, Marcy, had a meeting last week with another vendor. They had a lower price than you guys. Even though we're doctors, our practice runs on pretty tight margins. I'm just not sure we can afford you."

Scott nods his head. "Yes, I think I know which vendor you're referring to. In fact, just last month we had a group call us to switch over from them. Not that there is anything wrong with their service; it's just that the price can be misleading.

With us, everything is transparent. All of the installation, monthly service fees—everything—is included. That other group has a different pricing structure, so what looked like a lower price actually ended up being higher when all was said and done. Here, let me show you our service price list."

As Ed took the paper, he nodded and leaned in. *Good*, thought Scott. *I think we're close.*

Just then, though, someone walked in the room.

12. HANDLING THE DISCONNECT:
Prospects and Customers Who Are Different from You

"Is your mother home?" the salesman asked a small boy sitting on the steps in front of a house. "Yeah, she's home," the boy said, scooting over to let him past. The salesman rang the doorbell, got no response, knocked once, then again. Still no one came to the door. Turning to the boy, the fellow said, "I thought you said your mother was home." The kid replied, "She is, but this isn't where I live."

When Lynne decides to buy a car, she waits until she can afford a brand-new model. She doesn't like used cars. She selects the style and color first and then test-drives the vehicle once. If she likes the way it drives and it looks good to her aesthetically, the decision is all but made. Once she's responded on an emotional level, it's unlikely that she'll shop around for a different car. She only wants to work with a friendly, outgoing salesperson who likes to chat. Any hint of a pressured sales tactic, and she'll go to another dealer, because her mind is made up. Finally, if the car is in her price range and has a decent safety record, she'll probably make the purchase.

Dan only buys used cars that get great mileage. He reviews *Consumer Reports* to check out safety reports and equipment ratings. He will shop for months and test-drive several vehicles before he makes a purchase. He too is turned off by pushy salespeople and would rather be left alone when he's shopping. Only when he is ready to purchase will he approach a salesperson. Then he'll use data to negotiate the deal.

Because your customers have different styles, they are going to like different things, and this will influence their buying motivations. Chances are that you're going to encounter customers who have a different style than you in some key areas. This chapter will cover how to handle a disconnect between your style and that of your customer.

Communication Style

One of the most obvious differences between people are in communication style. There are widely different norms when it comes to gender, race, culture, geography, and even age. Imagine this scenario between twenty-five-year old Brittany and sixty-year-old Todd. She's a clerk in a music store.

Brittany: Hi! Can I help you?

Todd: Yes. I am looking for a record to play for some friends this evening.

Brittany (looking at his age and attire, she assumes that he'd be into classic rock): Umm, yeah. We have some Eagles over there. (She points to a rack of CDs.)

Todd: I said I was looking for a record. And I hate the Eagles. They're pedestrian and predictable pop.

Brittany (staring at him blankly): Yeah . . . Well, what *do* you like, then?

Todd: I find jazz to be a great expression of emotional range.

Brittany: Oh! You mean, like Billie Holiday? We have some of her old stuff over there.

Todd: No, not Billie Holiday. I'm more into Miles Davis, John Coltrane, and Thelonious Monk. But why do you keep pointing to CDs? Where are your *records*?

Brittany: Umm, I'm going on break. Let me get my manager to help you.

Gender Differences in Communication Style

Researcher Karima Merchant writes about how communication styles differ between men and women:*

---

* Karima Merchant, "How Men And Women Differ: Gender Differences in Communication Styles, Influence Tactics, and Leadership Styles." Claremont McKenna colleges, senior theses, paper 513 (2012): http://scholarship.claremont.edu/cmc_theses/513.

Gender differences in communication styles and influence tactics have created stereotypical gender roles that have affected the behaviors of both men and women in the workplace. . . .

The biggest difference between men and women and their style of communication boils down to the fact that *men and women view the purpose of conversations differently.* Academic research on psychological gender differences has shown that while women use communication as a tool to enhance social connections and create relationships, men use language to exert dominance and achieve tangible outcomes. . . . Women are, overall, more expressive, tentative, and polite in conversation, while men are more assertive, and power-hungry. . . . Men and women also differ in their relations towards others in society: while women strive to be more social in their interactions with others, men value their independence. On the other had, popular works by John Gray and Deborah Tannen show that while men view conversations as a way to establish and maintain status and dominance in relationships, women see the purpose of conversation to create and foster an intimate bond with the other party by talking about topical problems and issues they are communally facing. . . .

In John Gray's popular book *Men are from Mars, Women are from Venus: a Practical Guide for Improving Communication and Getting What You Want in a Relationship,* he outlines the underlying differences in communication styles between men and women. Gray's book is widely considered to be one of the most important benchmark pieces of literature on communication differences across gender of the twentieth century. . . .

The main differences Gray identifies between communication styles of men and women are as follows: Men are goal-oriented, they define their sense of self through their ability to achieve results. . . . Women, on the other hand, are relationship-oriented as they define their sense of self by their feelings and by the quality of their relationships. . . . Men and women also cope with stress differently; men cope by withdrawing themselves from the conversation or situation while women cope by reaching out and talking about the cause of their stress. Gray coined the phrase, "Men go their caves and women talk" to describe this psychological difference in coping with stress between men and women. . . . Overall, men want to feel needed, appreciated, and admired, while women strive to feel cherished, respected, and devoted. . . . Men and women also differ in their communication style when they are faced with resolving a crisis or coming to a mutual conclusion. The most common communicative mistake made by both males and females occurs when talking about and resolving conflict. When attempting to resolve a problem, men follow their natural tendency to offer a solution while women seek empathy and understanding and are naturally inclined to offer unsolicited advice. . . . These natural tendencies often create a rift between men when communicating with the opposite sex as men and women approach conversations differently.

Like John Gray, Deborah Tannen is also famous for her literature on differences in communication styles across gender. In 1990, Tannen wrote the book, *You Just Don't Understand: Women and Men in Conversation*, to explain the gender differences in communication styles between men and women. She found that these differences across gender start at a young age. Tannen noticed that boys create relationships with each other by doing things together; activities are central to their friendship. Girls, on the other hand, create close relationships with each other by simply talking, "talk is the essence of intimacy."

Of course, this is the twenty-first century. We've since discovered that it's not necessarily a matter of the biological gender of the communicators, but more of their style. There are men who have a more indirect style of communicating and women who have a more direct style. It's not so much the gender of the person that matters, but mirroring their communication style.

In our example above, Brittany and Todd got into a problem because (a) she had a more informal style than he did, and (b) she didn't understand her product well enough.

Differences in Decision Style

Another core area that is relevant to sales are the differences in decision-making style. An article in the *Harvard Business Review* has identified four key decision styles.* They take into account how much information a person uses when making a decision and how many options they tend to consider. Let's take a quick look at the key factors involved.

Information Use

Some people want to consider a lot of information and data before making any decision. They are called *maximizers*. These customers can't rest until they are certain they've found the very best answer. They'll come to a well-informed decision, but it can take a lot of time to wade through all the information.

Other people just want the key facts. They don't need as much information as maximizers to make a choice. These individuals are called *satisficers*, and are ready to act as soon as they have enough information to satisfy their emotional and cognitive requirements.

---

* Kenneth R. Brousseau, Mike Driver, Gary Hourihan, and Rikard Larsson, "The Seasoned Executive's Decision-Making Style," *Harvard Business Review*, Feb. 2006: http://hbr.org/2006/02/the-seasoned-executives-decision-making-style/ar/1.

Options

As far as the number of options goes, *single-focus* decision makers believe in taking and sticking to one course of action. *Multifocused* decision makers tend to generate lists of possible options and may pursue multiple courses of action.

Environmental Load

Another factor is at play too. It's called *environmental load*, which is a fancy name for stress or pressure. Do people tend to use more or less information when under increased environmental load? It depends. As the environmental load goes from low to moderate, they tend to use more information. But as environmental load goes from moderate to high, the amount of information used tends to fall off. This means that the closer you get to an important deadline or date, the less information your customer is going to want to use to make decisions.

Decision-Making Styles

Here are the four basic decision-making styles.

Decisive

Customers using the *decisive* style value action, speed, efficiency, and consistency. Once a plan is in place, they stick to it and move on to the next decision. In dealing with other people, they value honesty, clarity, loyalty, and especially brevity. In this mode, time is precious.

These customers tend to use low amounts of information and fewer numbers of options.

Decisive customers tend to know exactly what they want and expect you to find it for them. It can be frustrating to deal with them because they tend to be inflexible and avoid changing their minds.

Flexible

Like the decisive style, the *flexible* style focuses on speed, but here the emphasis is on adaptability. Faced with a problem, a person working in the flexible mode will get just enough information to solve the problem—and quickly change course if need be. These customers use lower amounts of information, but generate a greater number of options.

Flexible customers can be frustrating because they can be considered wishy-washy. They may tell you one thing and then come back a week later having changed their minds.

Hierarchic

Customers with a *hierarchic* style do not rush to judgment. Instead they analyze a great deal of information and expect others to contribute—and will readily challenge others' views, analyses, and decisions. This is the customer who will pore over the Internet and magazines making lists and comparing prices in order to narrow down options to the single best one. They use lots of information to generate a few options.

The frustrating thing about the hierarchic customer is that she believes there is one "perfect" solution to each purchasing decision. She'll search endlessly for the perfect option and will be reluctant to make a decision, because there might be something better out there.

Integrative

The *integrative* customer uses input from many different sources to generate as many options as possible: "I might want a white one, but would consider a black one as well." Their decisions can change as circumstances change.

Integrative customers can be frustrating because they take so long to make up their minds. You'll be ready for them to make a decision, but they won't be ready to make it just yet.

The more readily you can match your communication style to the decision-making style of your customers, the more effective you'll be at working with them. Make note of how much information they want to use in making choices, how many options they like to consider when making decisions, and how timely the decision is. This will help you understand the psychology of your customer so that you can avoid disconnects.

In the next chapter, we'll get into some of the reasons a sale can be lost at the last moment, and what you can do to avoid it.

SCOTT'S STORY

Scott and Ed were close to sealing the deal when the office door opened. In walked Linda Perkins, the administrator for the group of doctors. Closing the door behind her, she strutted over to the desk where Scott and Ed were sitting. She extended her hand, and Scott was surprised at how firm her handshake was. "Hi, I'm Linda," she said. "I run the practice. I understand you're here to talk about upgrading our IT systems?"

"That's correct. Ed and I were just . . ."

Linda interrupted, "I'm surprised you went and had this meeting without me. After all, as the administrator, I should be part of any decision that involves every employee in the practice."

Scott was taken aback. He understood Ed to be the sole decision maker. As he looked back and forth between Ed and Linda to see what would happen next, Ed sighed and leaned back, rubbing his head.

"Linda, we talked about this. Jeff and the others decided that in the interest of time, I would meet with the sales reps and make the final choice about which company to pursue."

Linda didn't like hearing that. "I know how you doctors are when it comes to making a decision. You don't consider enough information. You rush to judgment. You don't consider the feelings of anyone else."

Scott couldn't believe he was hearing this. Should he leave and let them work it out? Should he stay and counter

(continued)

Linda's objections? Should he just sit quietly and see what happens next?

Ed stood up and walked over to the door. Looking at Linda directly, he said, "Linda, this is neither the time nor the place for this conversation. I'll meet you in your office in fifteen minutes, and we can talk about this further." He opened the door, and Linda sheepishly walked out.

"I am so sorry about that," said Ed. "We've been having problems with her. I think she feels threatened that changing our IT systems to the cloud will take away some of her power, and we won't need her anymore. At any rate, I'm ready to proceed with using your company for this. I'm convinced."

Breathing an audible sigh of relief, Scott goes to his bag and pulls out the initial paperwork. Little does he know that Linda is not gone for long.

13. KNOW WHEN THE PARTY IS OVER:
How Not to Lose the Sale

An inexperienced real-estate salesman asked his boss if he could refund the deposit to an angry customer who had discovered that the lot he had bought was under water. "What kind of salesman are you?" the boss scolded. "Get out there and sell him a boat."

In a 2001 episode of the television show *Friends*, the character Monica buys a pair of fabulous boots. Her husband, Chandler, wants her to return them because they are too expensive: they cost even more than the rent. Monica, convinced she's going to love them, promises to wear them all the time and reassures him that they'll be worth the money.

However, the more Monica wears the boots, the more they hurt her feet. It gets to the point where she is in excruciating pain and is limping around. When another character asks why she doesn't just take them back, she says, "I can't! They have blood all inside them!"

Chandler has a Christmas party at his office, and he wants Monica to wear the boots because he thinks she loves them so much. She is too embarrassed to tell him that the boots are hurting her feet, so she wears them. We see the couple leaving the party. Monica is crying because there was dancing, and her feet hurt so badly she can barely walk. When Chandler suggests that they walk the fourteen blocks home, she confesses that she hates the boots. Chandler ends up carrying her all the way home.

This story line is an example of one way a sale can be lost after it's been closed. This chapter will cover some of the things you *don't* want to do, both during and after your sales presentation, as well as some ways to minimize buyer's remorse.

What *Not* to Do in Your Sales Presentation

Never read during your proposal. You may want to quote from a book or an article, but don't do this for more than a sentence or two. Unless you are very experienced at reading aloud, your voice will put people to sleep in short order.

Once you've made your points, *don't feel you have to keep talking just to fill up the time.* Speakers get in trouble when their selling points aren't clear to the speakers themselves, so they keep trying to elaborate and clarify. Make sure you can state your benefits in a few clear sentences as you prepare your presentation. The rest of what you say should amplify that message, not explain it. Give them key points that they can grasp easily, and *eliminate conflicting messages.* Use vocabulary everyone can understand.

Minimize jargon. Every industry and specialization has it. On the one hand, using appropriate jargon or industry language shows that you're an insider. On the other hand, it's easy to overdo. Too much comes across as either trying too hard to be viewed as an insider or as an inability to speak in a way that a general audience can understand.

Don't look down, but don't look up either. Keep your eyes off the floor and off the ceiling too. Nerves can cause presenters to avoid eye contact with the very people they want to engage. This makes your listeners feel left out on a personal level, so it's unlikely they will invest in you professionally.

Convey information with variety in your voice, energetic body language, and authentic enthusiasm. Be dynamic! Believe in your product, and let the buyers know how much you believe in it. Passion is contagious. It's more convincing than logic. Whether your presentation is "perfect" or not, if you are passionate about it, the message will come across.

Stop talking when you've made the sale. Once the prospect says yes, resist the temptation to keep selling. You might undo what you've already done.

Avoid lecturing. There is a fine line between impressing others with your knowledge and boring them to tears with a recitation from on high. What are the signs that you may be lecturing rather than educating? First, watch for long periods of uninterrupted talking time. Just how long have you been droning on? It's likely to be longer than you think. This is why you want to pause frequently, with short comments to ensure your listener is still with you. Sometimes you might use a question: "Can you guess what happened next?" Other times you will want to check for understanding. "Is that making sense?" If you catch yourself thinking, "Have I been talking for too long?" the likely answer is, "Yes, I have."

Buyer's Remorse

Just like Monica with her boots, often customers will experience regret or remorse after they've agreed to the sale. It's exacerbated when the item purchased is expensive, like a car* or a house. It may stem from fear of making the wrong choice, guilt over extravagance, or a suspicion of having been overly influenced by the seller.

Buyer's remorse† is thought to stem from something called *postdecision dissonance*. This mental state occurs when a person has to choose between two similar alternatives. One common example is when you order dinner at a restaurant; then the waiter walks by with something that looks better, and you think, "I should have gotten that instead."

According to Wikipedia, factors that affect buyer's remorse include resources invested, the involvement of the purchaser, whether the purchase is compatible with the purchaser's goals, and evidence encountered post-

---

* Gerard D. Bell, "The Automobile Buyer after the Purchase," *Journal of Marketing* 31, no. 3 (July 1967): 12–16.

† "Buyer's Remorse," Wikipedia (website), last updated Sept. 12, 2019: https://en.wikipedia.org/wiki/Buyer's_remorse.

purchase that either confirms or denies that it was a good idea.

Before the purchase, buyers often feel positive emotions toward it. They're excited about it; they can't wait to use it. Because the mind doesn't like dissonance, they tend to minimize the product's negative aspects. "That blue isn't such a bad color."

Moreover, before the purchase, buyers still have all the options. They've still got their money. They can still pick any of the available choices. They can even choose not to buy.

But things change once you buy.

After you've made the decision, you're more able to experience its negative aspects. "I really don't like that blue. I should have gotten the white one." Now your only options are to either return the item or keep it, even if you no longer want it.

Another thing that can contribute to buyer's remorse is the worry that someone else might judge the purchase or suggest a better alternative: "You should have come to me! I could have gotten you a white one for less money!"

How Remorseful Are You?

The following table was developed by Sweeney, Hausknecht, and Soutar in a study to investigate three elements (one emotional, two cognitive) of buyer's remorse.*

---

* Jillian Sweeney, Douglas Hausknecht, and Geoffrey Soutar, "Cognitive Dissonance after Purchase: A Multidimensional Scale," *Psychology and Marketing* 17, no. 5 (May 2000): 369–85.

Elements of cognitive dissonance (Twenty-Two Items)	
	After I bought this product:
Emotional	I was in despair.
	I resented it.
	I felt disappointed with myself.
	I felt scared.
	I felt hollow.
	I felt angry.
	I felt uneasy.
	I felt I'd let myself down.
	I felt annoyed.
	I felt frustrated.
	I was in pain.
	I felt depressed.
	I felt furious with myself.
	I felt sick.
	I was in agony.
Wisdom of purchase	I wonder if I really need this product.
	I wondered whether I should have bought anything at all.
	I wondered if I had made the right choice.
	I wondered if I had done the right thing in buying this product.
Concern over deal	I wondered if I'd been fooled.
	I wondered if they had spun me a line.
	I wondered whether there was something wrong with the deal I got.

Relieving Remorse

Obviously, as a salesperson you don't want your customers to be feeling any of these things after the close of the sale. Is there anything you can do to prevent or minimize buyer's remorse?

Clearly, one thing is to not sell people products that they don't really need or want. But having gone through the steps in this book, you're not likely to fall into that problem.

Buyer's remorse can be reduced by post-purchase confirmation.* If there is follow-up paperwork, don't just email it to the client. Do it face-to-face, or by phone if necessary. This way you can pick up on any signs of post-decision regret and counter it.

Another way to do it is to encourage the customer to return. This can be in the form of a coupon for future use. This has many benefits for both the consumer and retailer. First, the consumer is more likely to return to the store with the coupon, which will result in a higher percentage of repeat customers. Each successive time a purchase is made and is deemed satisfactory, buyer's remorse is less likely to be experienced. Customers can justify their purchases with product performance.†

Another technique used is the money-back guarantee: a guarantee from the retailer that the product will

---

* Ronald Milliman and Philip Decker, "The Use of Post-purchase Communication to Reduce Dissonance and Improve Direct Marketing Effectiveness," Journal of Business Communication 27, no. 2 (1990): 159–70.

† M. Nadeem, "Post-purchase Dissonance: The Wisdom of the 'Repeat' Purchases," Journal of Global Business Issues 1, no. 2 (2007): 183–93.

meet the customer's needs or the customer is entitled to a full refund. This technique is highly successful at lessening buyer's remorse, because it immediately makes the decision a changeable one. The unchangeability of an all-sales-final purchase can lead to a larger amount of psychological discomfort at the point of the decision.* This makes the stakes higher, and poor choices will cause significant buyer's remorse.

Again, it all boils down to having a relationship. If you're focused on building an ongoing relationship with your customers, they'll have a greater level of trust with you, so they can tell you if they're not happy.

* John Tierney, "A Cure for Buyer's Remorse," *The New York Times*, Tierney Lab (website), Nov. 7, 2007: https://tierneylab.blogs.nytimes.com/2007/11/07/a-cure -for-buyers-remorse/?_r=0.

Scott's Story

Scott was out taking his Rottweiler, Carl, for his morning run when his cell phone rang. He let it go to voicemail, because he didn't want an eighty-pound dog dragging him along while he was trying to talk to a client. When he listened to the message, he heard Ed's voice. "Scott, We have a problem. Linda is going ballistic that I signed the paperwork with you, and she's got the other doctors questioning the decision. I'm sorry to say this, but I think we're going to have to hold off on this for a while. At least until we can get Linda calmed down."

Shaking his head, Scott hit "return call" on his phone. As it was ringing, he could envision Linda complaining.

"Ed," he said, "it's Scott. I got your message."

"Yeah, sorry. Things are just escalating with her."

"Not to worry. I actually deal with this all the time. How about this? What if I came into the office tomorrow at lunch, and we have a Taco 'bout It Tuesday meeting? This way Linda and the rest of the doctors can ask me questions and share their objections face-to-face. Sound good?"

"I like that idea a lot. I'll let everyone know, and we'll see you tomorrow."

Later the next day, as Scott was driving back to the office after meeting with the doctors, he reflected back on the experience. He was glad that Ed allowed him back to talk with everyone and ease their concerns. The little bit of extra effort it took to have that meeting made the difference between keeping and losing the sale. And the tacos didn't hurt.

Step Four
Parting Gifts

Planning

Product Knowledge

Customer Understanding

Competition Management

Getting Ready

Seller's Needs and Wants

Buyer's Needs and Wants

Opening the Door/ Closing the Sale

Healthy Sales Relationship

Parting Gifts/ Follow-Up

14. FOLLOW-UP, FEEDBACK, AND REFERRALS

Life insurance agent to would-be client: "Don't let me frighten you into a hasty decision. Sleep on it tonight. If you wake up in the morning, give me a call then and let me know."

You've done it! You've made the sale. Now it's time to sit back, celebrate, and move on, right? Not so fast. If you do that, you're missing out on a huge component of relationship selling—the relationship! The goal here is to create a healthy sales relationship that outlasts any single transaction. Even if you're just selling fast-food hamburgers, you want the customer to come back time and time again.

Think about it. You wouldn't go on one date and then stop seeing the other person because you had a good time. You wouldn't take a friend to the movies and then never go again because you both liked the movie so much. Opening the door and closing the sale doesn't mean you never open the door again. In fact, it's just the opposite.

In any sales endeavor, acquiring first-time customers is a major expense in time, effort, and money. But once you satisfactorily deliver your product or service and have a core customer base, you can continuously rework and resell at a very modest cost per sale. When you have a database of customers who have already invested in your products or services, it costs very little to go to them with additional offers.

Keep in Touch

Always take advantage of an opportunity to stay in touch with your buyers. You can:
- Write personal notes or letters
- Send a gift or a gift certificate
- Mail holiday or greeting cards
- Send a simple email asking if there's anything you can provide to them

Dropping the F-Bomb

In his book *7L: The Seven Levels of Communication*, author Michael Maher offers a comprehensive system for following up with customers and prospects so that they can move up the customer continuum. It's called the *F-bomb*, and the letter F stands for *follow-up*.

The F-bomb is a system for follow-up that you'll create for your one-on-one meetings: a seven-week series of POWER notes, direct mail pieces, emails, and phone calls. At least four of your follow-up touches need to be phone calls. Use your CRM or calendar to schedule these tasks. The key, Maher says, is to communicate with your customers and prospects intentionally and on a schedule rather than when you feel like it.

A Heart to Help

Now you might be wondering, "That's a lot of follow-up. What will I say to these people that's not annoying?" It can range from the casual, "Just calling to see how you're doing with the product" to a direct-mail piece about a new product you're adding to the line. You can send them success stories of other customers who've used the product.

After every call, rank yourself on a 0 to 10 scale: how happy was the person to hear from you? Zero means they hung up on you, and 10 means it was like reconnecting with your best friend. You want people to look at the caller ID, see that it's you, and be excited to answer the phone.

The way to get people to look forward to your call is to help them. Call with a heart to help. They may need contractors' information, the location for a vendor, a job recommendation, or whatever. You can take the time after the call to get them whatever they need. In the meantime, you're connecting them to your referral partners, strategic allies, and other people who can help them. Their network grows bigger. When you help others, your community grows stronger.

Maher also recommends that salespeople write a "power note" to leads and customers as part of the F-bomb strategy. These are handwritten notes (not typed) and are sent by traditional mail.

Seven Steps to a POWER Note

1. Use unbranded cards with a symbol or monogram that represents you. It's a personal note.

2. Use blue ink. It looks original and positive.

3. Words: use *you*, but avoid *I, me, my*.

4. Be specific in your praise. Identify and acknowledge a characteristic, a talent, a unique quality.

5. Leverage the power of positive projection. Identify a personal characteristic you want to improve and express respect for others who possess that quality (happiness, wealth, balance, etc.)

6. Write right: slope text slightly upward from left to right.

7. The power of the P.S.: Use a P.S. as a call to action: ask the recipient to take action such as emailing or calling.

As mentioned, you should include success stories and testimonials. Maher offers some tips on creating a success story with impact.

Seven Steps to a Successful Success Story

1. What was the client's name and situation? Be specific about the problem or challenge. For example: Josh and Jill were first-time home buyers.

2. What would have happened if you weren't involved? (What is the worst thing that could have happened? Josh and Jill could have bought the first home they saw—backing up onto a highway.)

3. How did you help them solve the problem? (Educated them on what makes a good investment.)

4. What was the result? Be specific. (They bought a great home that is a great investment. On a cul-de-sac, with a desirable plan, and in a neighborhood that has a good history of appreciation.)

5. What did the client say or do to let you know you did well? (Include their testimonial or mention that they referred you. For example, "They referred me to Chris Hills, another first-time home buyer.")

6. Ask for *specific* and *relevant* referrals. Example: whom do you know who is buying their first home? (It could be a renter or even a son or daughter of someone the client knows.)

7. Call to action. Use a sentence like: "Please reply to this email with the name and their situation. I promise they'll get the excellent service they deserve."

Maher recommends creating twelve success stories and sending them out once a month to your list. That's how you continually communicate your solutions to your community without being overbearing or annoying.

> *Remember, success attracts success.*
> *—Michael Maher*

You can see that these communications serve two purposes: they keep you in touch with your customers, but they also serve as a bridge to referrals.

The Door-to-Door Method of Referral Generation (Hint: It's Not What You Think)

Asking for a referral can make people unnecessarily uncomfortable. A referral is like an emotionally charged endorsement: someone puts his reputation on the line for you. It's easier for a person to introduce you to a friend than refer you. A connection is just what it sounds like: someone putting you in touch with an individual you should meet. It's about finding people who, like you, would appreciate the same service or product.

Michael Maher recommends that you tell your customers this: "I ask you that when you see, hear, or meet a person who mentions my service, that you give them my card and give me a call. My promise to you is that I will respond quickly to determine how I can help them. Would you do that for me, please?"

Look for opportunities to have somebody else sing your praises, introduce you to someone they know, or connect you to a connector. Maher calls this the *triangle of trust*. The book *Listen* refers to it as *Heider's balance theory*.

In 1946, theorist Fritz Heider developed *balance theory* to examine relationships between people and things.* It can be best visualized as a triangle, with the points labeled P (person), O (other), and X (a third element).

---

* "Balance Theory," Wikipedia (website), updated Jan. 18, 2020: https://en.wikipedia.org/wiki/Balance_theory.

When this state is balanced, all three elements have a positive association with each other. When your customer shares his positive impression of you with her friend, the friend is more likely to have a positive impression of you too.

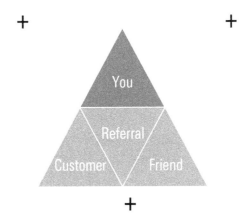

This is the power of referrals. It's like going door-to-door in a neighborhood, but getting the neighbors to invite you in because they already like what you're selling.

Once you develop a systematized routine for contacting your leads and clients, it will become second nature. You'll be watching TV and handwriting notes. You'll set aside fifteen minutes at the beginning and end of every day to make calls. You'll eat your lunch at your desk twice a week while writing follow-up emails. You'll be amazed at the results.

SCOTT'S STORY

"Hi, Scott? My name is Mike Savoy. Ed Lewis gave me your number. I'm his veterinarian, actually, and we are looking to upgrade our IT to the cloud. He loves what you guys did for him, and I was wondering if maybe we could set up a meeting."

Scott loves to get messages like that. It's been about six months since he met with Ed and his company converted Ed's office to SAAS and cloud-based IT. The process went seamlessly, and even Linda is happy with the end result.

Scott's system of following up with his customers and leads has been more effective than he ever dreamed. It only takes a few minutes, but his close rate has gone up (he is calculating that monthly now, remember?) because the leads he's getting are already warm. A full 50 percent of his new business comes from referrals. That's practically free money in his pocket! Even better, he's developed a bunch of friendships with his customers that are personally satisfying and enriching.

CONCLUSION
The Future of Selling

"This house," said the real estate salesperson, "has both its good points and its bad points. To show you I'm honest, I'm going to tell you about both. The disadvantages are that there is a chemical plant one block south and a landfill a block north."

"What are the advantages?" inquired the prospective buyer.

"The advantage is that you can always tell which way the wind is blowing."

Every profession must change to keep up with the times. There's an old saying that even if your company makes the best buggy whip, your salespeople still won't be able to sell them, because no one has buggies anymore. Times change. Products change. Sales is changing too.

A Change in the Wind

Sales is one of those universal skills that is easy to apply across industries. But there is a definite change in the wind when it comes to selling. Recently Sandeep Chatterjee, founder and CEO of the Emerging Ventures

Platform, or EVx, wrote an article on the changing future of sales.* He said:

> Technological advances are making it easier and faster to translate ideas into commercial products. For example, new software tools and programming languages allow for the development of software systems in a matter of days instead of months. Physical goods can also be readily fabricated or manufactured. In fact, 3D printers will soon bring manufacturing directly into our homes and offices.
>
> In line with this trend, the true value of a product or service is becoming more about its underlying idea and less about its implementation. In this context, larger companies typically have the operational and marketing capabilities to translate ideas into commercial products and to bring them to market quickly and cost-effectively. What these companies may lack, however, is a steady flow of good ideas to generate value in a sustainable way. Many individuals, on the other hand, including college students, professors and professionals, have great ideas but lack the means or know-how to commercialize them. How can these often brilliant ideas be harnessed? What needs to be done to connect these ingenious and cre-

---

* Sandeep Chatterjee, "Selling Ideas: The Future of Jobs," WIPO magazine (website), Feb. 2016: http://www.wipo.int/wipo_magazine/en/2016/01/article_0007.html.

ative individuals with the companies that have the interest and the means to bring their ideas to market?

Redefining the Problem

Ago Cluytens, practice director at RAIN Group, writes:

Those new ideas and perspectives revolve not only around how to solve the problem, but very often provide a new take on how to define the problem in the first place. . . .

But in an approach that is mostly focused on ideas, generating new insights and perspectives and reframing a buyer's mindset and points of view, the value essentially originates from the conversations that are being had between buyers and sellers.

In this approach, it is *the seller who becomes the value*. . . .

Already, buyers are turning increasingly to the power of the Internet and social media to conduct research, help define the problem, and develop a deeper understanding of their needs, as well as "vet" potential vendors.

In the future, we expect that trend to continue and strengthen.

Those sellers who act as deep generalists, redefine their buyers realities, deliver value through their interactions on a day-to-day basis and uncover new forms of unexpected impact are increasingly likely to do so to a variety of communication channels, from live meetings to conference calls to online chat.*

KPIs of the Future

What does all this mean for the average salesperson? It means that your value in the sales process isn't going to be grounded in a product or service. Anyone can order shoes online at 2:00 a.m. They can do their own research and find their own options. They don't need a salesperson for that anymore. They need someone who can help them see things differently. You're not just selling shoes. You're helping your customer identify her values and her self-image and then find shoes along those lines. If she's vegan, let her know about the latest trends in vegan footwear. If she's an athlete, talk with her about new fabric for shoes.

The salesperson who will succeed in this new environment is the one who brings a steady flow of creative ideas to the table and can help customers midwife their great ideas from the mind into something that's commercially viable.

What, then, are the KPIs that future salespeople might measure?

---

* Ago Cluytens, "The Future of Consultative Selling: Seven Shifts That Make Sales Success Inevitable," PersistIQ (website), accessed May 23, 2020: https://persistiq.com/blog/the-future-of-consultative-selling-7-shifts-that-make-sales-success-inevitable/.

- Number of related books read per month
- Creative thinking exercises conducted
- Number of client problems solved
- Customer satisfaction
- Number of referrals
- Number of social media platforms and frequency of engagement

Relationships Will Matter Even More

All this is telling us that relationship selling skills will become even more important as time goes on. The next generation of people are likely to be called the Social Generation, as they interact with each other in innovative ways.

To keep up, you need to up your game. Stay on the cutting edge. Read. Learn. Grow. Most importantly, never forget that sales is, at its heart, a matter between two people.

Key Takeaways

- In order for the sales relationship to be balanced, it has to accommodate both the perspective of the salesperson and the buyer. If either one becomes dominant, the sales relationship topples.
- The true modern sales cycle has more in common with event planning than with a traditional sales cycle.

- Like in event planning, the salesperson needs to be able to create an *experience* for the customer. It's not only about having the best product. It's also about the experience of buying.

- The sales relationship is about understanding the needs and wants of both the seller and the buyer and finding that sweet spot in the middle.

- Calls, emails, and follow-up notes can keep the relationship going and make it far more likely that the customer will choose your business again.

- RAID is a feedforward technique that helps you start with the results desired and then develop a strategy to achieve them.

- Deep product knowledge can help you transform features into benefits.

- In order to sell someone your product or service, you have to understand how it benefits them. Knowing your product is the first half. Knowing your customer avatar is the second.

- Use the two-qualifier method to identify your ideal customer:
  [QUALIFIER 1] + [QUALIFIER 2] who need **[YOUR SERVICE]**

- If you're to sell competitively, you need to fully understand your competition's strengths and weaknesses as well as opportunities and threats.

- The link between an internal locus of control (a belief), bias for action (an inclination to act), and actually making a sale is in the actions that a person takes.

- Key performance indicators (KPIs) are the activities you must perform to achieve success. They focus on tasks and behaviors that are easily quantifiable.
- Cold calling doesn't work.
- Brand yourself as an expert at what you sell.
- Understanding your needs and wants in the sales relationship is a good foundation for successful sales.
- In life, it's not possible to avoid being rejected. For some, it's the fuel that fires them on to greatness.
- Therefore it's important to consciously look at the frame you have for sales rejection and the filter you use to receive it. Then you can change the filter to one that allows you to experience rejection differently.
- A masterful use of rapport can convert skeptical prospects into paying clients.
- One of the most important keys is not the question you ask, but how engaged you are as a listener.
- The single best thing you can do to improve your presentation skills is to practice telling stories.
- This is the magic formula:
  Incident: Describe the customer's situation before implementing your solution.
  Action: Explain how your solution was implemented.
  Benefit: Emphasize how your solution created value for the customer.
- The key to a successful offer is to focus on the benefits that match the buyer's specific needs.

- Only give enough consultation to tell the client how you would solve the problem. Don't solve it for them before they've committed to buy.
- By being aware of the signals you're getting, you'll know whether or not to advance the conversation to the ask or retreat to handle objections.
- Commitment doesn't mean only asking for the order. It's much broader than that. It can be asking for the next meeting or setting a time for the next phone call or faxed document.
- Objections are just part of the decision-making process.
- People buy from different perspectives. These perspectives depend on personalities and vary by function. Make sure you sell to people on the basis of their needs and their points of view.
- The first step in overcoming objections is to *create some level of cooperation between the buyer and yourself.*
- Any product marketed with low price as the unique selling proposition will always be vulnerable.
- The more readily you can match your communication style to your customers' decision-making style, the more effective you'll be at working with them. Note how much information they want to use in making choices, how many options they like to consider when making decisions, and how timely the decision is.
- Buyer's remorse can be reduced by post-purchase confirmation.

- If you're focused on building an ongoing relationship with your customers, they'll have a greater level of trust with you and are more likely to tell you if they're not happy.
- Always take advantage of an opportunity to stay in touch with your buyers.
- Look for opportunities to have somebody else sing your praises, introduce you to someone they know, or connect you to a connector.
- The salesperson who will succeed in the future is the one who brings a steady flow of creative ideas to the table and can help customers midwife their great ideas into something that's commercially viable.

CPSIA information can be obtained
at www.ICGtesting.com
Printed in the USA
JSHW011315110820
7238JS00005B/70